1

Printed in the United States of America

Table of Contents

Total Rewards

Training and Development

Employee and Labor Relations

Risk Management

Disclaimer

This is an unofficial study guide for the PHR/SPHR certification exam and is not endorsed by the Society for Human Resource Management or HR Certification Institute. The information contained in this study guide is of a general nature and is intended to help HR professionals review the broad body of knowledge required for PHR/SPHR certification. While this guide intends to provide a broad overview of all HR competencies, there is no guarantee that all of the terms, concepts, and information in this guide will appear on the exam(s), and likewise, that all of the questions asked on the actual exam(s) are covered by this guide. Finally, there is no guarantee, express or implied, that studying this guide will lead to your passage of the exam(s). You are advised to do your own, independent research on the current requirements and guidelines of the PHR/SPHR certification exam and use this guide as a tool.

Introduction

Congratulations on taking a step closer to becoming a certified human resources professional! The HR Certification Institute, established in 1976, is an internationally recognized certifying organization for the HR profession. To date, HRCI has certified over 130,000 HR professionals across the globe based on a combination of experience and examination. HR certification is a globally recognized demonstration of professional achievement.

HRCI offers different types of certification exams for the HR profession including Professional in Human Resources (PHR), Senior Professional in Human Resources (SPHR), Global Professional in Human Resources (GPHR), and more. This study guide focuses on preparing candidates for PHR and SPHR certifications[1].

PHR Certification

According to HRCI, the Professional in Human Resources (PHR) certification requires mastery of the tactical aspects of HR, and a foundational knowledge of U.S. laws and regulations. The credential is geared for the HR professional who implements HR programs, acts tactically, reports to a more senior HR professional, and focuses on the HR department rather the entire organization[2].

SPHR Certification

The Senior Professional in Human Resources (SPHR®) certification, according to HRCI, is intended for those who demonstrate mastery of strategic HR management. It is designed for the HR professional who designs programs, focuses on the "big picture," is in charge of the HR department, and has a deep knowledge of all HR functions. SPHR candidates collaborate with organizational leaders and designs system-wide programs[3].

---

[1] Source: http://www.hrci.org/docs/default-source/web-files/2014-certification-handbook-pdf.pdf?sfvrsn=8

[2] Source: http://www.hrci.org/our-programs/our-hr-certifications/phr

[3] Source: http://www.hrci.org/our-programs/our-hr-certifications/sphr

Eligibility Requirements

Both certifications have different basic requirements. The following are the requirements listed by HRCI as of 2014:

PHR	SPHR
• At least one year of experience in an exempt-level (professional) HR position with a Master's degree or higher, OR	• At least four years of experience in an exempt-level (professional) HR position with a Master's degree or higher, OR
• At least two years of experience in an exempt-level (professional) HR position with a Bachelor's degree, OR	• At least five years of experience in an exempt-level (professional) HR position with a Bachelor's degree, OR
• At least four years of experience in an exempt-level (professional) HR position with a high school diploma	• At least seven years of experience in an exempt-level (professional) HR position with a high school diploma

Core Knowledge Required

HRCI designs each certification exam based on knowledge determined by HR practitioners around the world. HR tasks and the knowledge needed to perform them are extensively researched and grouped into functional areas. Below is the general body of knowledge required for the PHR/SPHR exams as of 2014, according to HRCI[4]:

PHR	SPHR
• Business Management and Strategy (11%)	• Business Management and Strategy (30%)
• Workforce Planning and Employment (24%)	• Workforce Planning and Employment (17%)
• Human Resource Development (18%)	• Human Resource Development (19%)
• Compensation and Benefits (19%)	• Compensation and Benefits (13%)
• Employee and Labor Relations (20%)	• Employee and Labor Relations (14%)
• Risk Management (8%)	• Risk Management (7%)

---

[4] Source: http://www.hrci.org/docs/default-source/web-files/phr_sphr-body-of-knowledge-pdf.pdf?sfvrsn=2

Exam Format

The PHR and SPHR exams are offered through computer-based testing proctored by Prometric, a professional test delivery company. Each exam consists of 175 multiple-choice questions, of which 150 are scored, and 25 are pre-test (unscored). Each question lists four possible answers, only one of which is correct. The time limit is 3 hours.

You will receive a preliminary result by Prometric after you complete the computer-based exam. HRCI will send your official results and score to you within 2-4 weeks, which indicates whether you passed or failed the exam. A scaled score of at least 500 is needed to pass.

Taking the Exam

- Be sure to register for an exam by the established deadlines listed at www.hrci.org.

- Give yourself several weeks to study and develop a study schedule to break up the information into manageable chunks.

- Find a study group or have a friend quiz you on HR knowledge.

- Get acquainted with the testing facility rules and check-in procedures located at www.prometric.com/hrci.

- On the night before an exam, get plenty of rest. Eat a full meal on the morning of the exam.

- Give yourself plenty of time to find the test site. Plan to arrive early.

- Arrive at least 30 minutes prior to your scheduled exam time. Bring a valid, government-issued photo ID.

Strategic HR Management

Section Overview

- → What is strategic management, and why is it important?
- → How are organizations structured and designed?
- → What are the main functions within most organizations?
- → What external factors affect how an organization is run?
- → How do organizations develop and change over time?
- → What is the strategic planning process, and what does it achieve?
- → How is HR involved in the strategic planning process?
- → How do organizations manage change?
- → How do companies ensure that their practices are ethical?
- → What is organizational design, and how does it affect decision-making?
- → What are the different approaches to leadership?
- → What is the role of human resources in the organization?
- → What is the difference between a generalist and a specialist?
- → How can HR professionals collaborate with business leaders?
- → Why do organizations develop HR policies and procedures?
- → How do HR professionals use technology to accomplish their goals and objectives?
- → How do HR professionals use data analysis to collaborate with leadership?
- → What is the role of HR in mergers and acquisitions?

What is Strategic Management?

Over the past century, companies have grown larger and more complicated as the demands of consumers and the business environment have changed and grown more complex and nuanced. Where the production of goods historically involved only a single worker, products are now created through multiple workers and machines. Additionally, as the U.S. economy has evolved from primarily manufacturing products to providing services, companies have needed to evolve to keep up with demand and trends in order to stay competitive. Over time, companies have developed new processes, restructured their personnel, adopted new tools, and reevaluated management practices to ensure that their employees are able to achieve these overarching goals.

To stay competitive in a continually evolving global marketplace, business leaders must be able to respond and adapt quickly to changes in conditions of the industry, economy, workforce, and regulatory environment. They need to be able to stay apprised of the needs of their clients and customers, and develop useful products and services to meet their demands. Successful business leaders are continually scanning the environment, making predictions, and developing business plans accordingly to stay on top of competition. This ongoing process of creation, research, reassessment, and development is called **strategic management.** Strategic management is important to HR professionals because it affects how HR can add value to the organization through policies, procedures, and programs.

Strategic HR management, then, is achieved when HR leaders and practitioners closely align themselves with the overall strategic management of the company. Since organizations are comprised of people, the human resources function is affected by everything that affects all people in the organization. When the organization must respond to changes in the marketplace, industry, or regulatory environment, HR practitioners are responsible for aligning the organization's people, policies, and processes with these changes. To be successful in doing so, they must collaborate with business leadership to stay aligned with business goals, objectives, and strategic vision.

Various Structures of Organizations

Every company is organized differently depending on the industry, size, tax implications, leadership, and other factors. However, all businesses operating in the United States are formally organized into these basic structures[5]:

- *Sole Proprietorships* - the most basic business structure in which the business owner operates alone. The business owner is the sole responsible party for the business (including finances) and has the sole authority in making business decisions. Any profits made by the business are the owner's, and the owner is personally responsible for all debts and liabilities of the company. Many business owners of a sole proprietorship operate the company through an assumed name registered with the county or state in which they operate.

- *Partnerships* - a business structure in which two or more people share ownership. Partnerships may take various forms, such as a general partnership, limited liability partnership, and joint venture, depending on the structure of ownership as well as the intended duration of the partnership. Many partnerships have formal agreements that outline how profits will be divided, how disputes will be resolved, how change in ownership may occur, and how the partnership may be dissolved.

- *Corporations* - a legal entity that is owned by shareholders (in the form of stock/equity), most commonly formed for large businesses. Unlike sole proprietorships and partnerships, the corporation itself (not the shareholders/owners) is liable for the actions and debts of the business. Shareholders are typically not involved in the day-to-day operations of the business. Instead, they elect a board of directors to represent their interests, and the company's senior leadership team makes decisions about the direction of the company.

- *Limited Liability Companies* - a hybrid between a partnership and a corporation. LLCs provide the liability protections of a corporation while offering the simplified tax implications of a partnership. The "owners" of an LLC are called "members," and depending on the state, there can be one or more members.

Operational Functions in an Organization[6]

Regardless of the size and formal structure of the organization (e.g., Corporation, LLC, partnership), there are common functions that can be found within almost every organization. Whether an organization offers products or services (depending on its objective or purpose), it must first develop its offerings and undergo various activities to deliver them to customers.

---

[5] Source: US Small Business Administration, http://www.sba.gov/category/navigation-structure/starting-managing-business/starting-business/choose-your-business-stru

[6] Source: Bureau of Labor Statistics, http://www.bls.gov/opub/mlr/2008/12/art3full.pdf

Below are the general functions of businesses that are all involved in some way with achieving the organization's objective:

- *Procurement, Logistics, and Distribution:* Acquiring resources (inputs) and delivering final products to customers.

- *Product/Service Development:* Designing, revising, and improving products or services offered to the marketplace; may include research, design, analysis, and engineering.

- *Operations:* Brings together raw products and production processes to create a final product or service; determines methods for cost savings.

- *Marketing and Sales:* Prospecting new buyers of services and developing/maintaining relationships with existing customers; promotes and advertises products and services through multiple channels.

- *Customer Service:* Typically supports customers after purchasing products or services; troubleshoots issues, resolves complaints, and answers questions about products or services.

The following are support services:

- *General Management:* Handles the corporate governance, accounting, facilities, management, and administrative support.

- *Human Resources:* Oversees the recruitment, hiring, training, compensation, and termination of employees.

- *Information Technology:* Maintains, automates, and designs technical infrastructure of the organization, including equipment, hardware, and software.

Depending on the complexity and size of the organization, these functions may be handled by one person or multiple people. All are necessary components for conducting business.

The External Environment

Regularly monitoring and responding to the external environment is critical to the success of an organization. External forces, such as the economy, consumer demand, laws and regulations, technology, and the labor force can greatly affect the operations of an organization. Being proactive and adapting to these changes accordingly can help an organization remain strong.

- *Economic conditions:* The economy affects all people, and therefore all businesses, in some way. When the economy is strong, consumers are able to afford more products and services, and therefore companies can thrive if they meet the demands of consumers. During economic prosperity, companies often innovate new products and services, and often expand their staff in order to meet demand. On the other hand, when the economy is stagnant or on the decline, consumers are purchasing fewer products and services. In this case, companies may respond by reducing production costs to offset the loss of profits.

- *Consumer demand:* Over time, consumers develop new tastes, attitudes, and behaviors. Much of this can be influenced by popular culture, mass media, social media, and advertising. What may have been useful for consumers a decade ago may not meet the same needs today. Therefore, to meet consumer demands, companies are often refining their existing products and services, as well as developing new ones.

- *Legal landscape:* New laws and regulations are regularly implemented by local, state, and federal governments and agencies. These laws and regulations can dictate how a company compensates employees, treats employees, and operates. Depending on where the company conducts business, it may have to follow rules in many different locations and therefore keep up with the changing legal landscape in each place.

- *Technology:* Throughout history, technology has transformed how business is conducted. The computer, for instance, revolutionized how companies interact internally and externally, and caused information and transactions to flow more freely and quickly. Keeping up with new and changing technology is advantageous for organizations, as technology often helps to streamline operations and increase efficiency.

- *Workforce:* A common saying among HR professionals is that an organization is only as good as its people. Therefore, it is in the best interests of the organization to attract the most qualified people to fulfill its goals. The talent and skills of the individuals within the available workforce is critical to the success of organizations everywhere.

Like people, organizations have their own life cycles. They are "born" (established), they develop and mature, they decline, and sometimes they "die" (dissolve). Just like people, as organizations mature, they begin to understand the environment around them, develop knowledge and wisdom, and plan for the future. Research has shown that organizations at any stage of the life cycle are impacted by both internal and external factors. In order to survive, an organization must be able to adapt to changes, demands, and their internal and external environment.

As an organization progresses through the life cycle and grows in size, its functions and features evolve over time, according to researcher Richard L. Daft[7]:

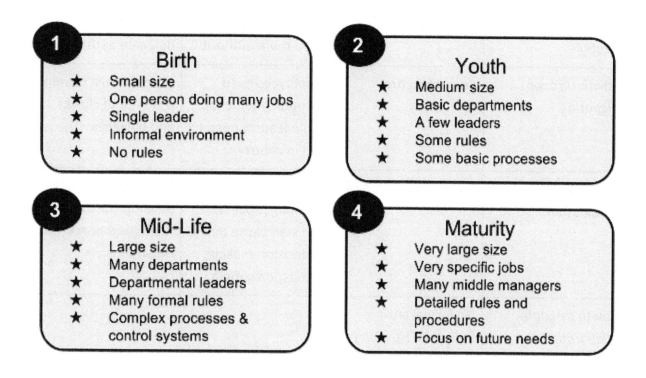

Growth Phases

In 1972, organizational development author Larry E. Greiner conceptualized five growth phases an organization undergoes: growth through direction; growth through delegation; growth through coordination; and growth through collaboration. According to his research, each

---

[7] Source: Free Management Library, http://managementhelp.org/organizations/life-cycles.htm

growth phase experiences an evolutionary phase (developing existing structure) of four to eight years, followed by a period of organizational crisis. The phases and the expected crises that result, according to his theory, are listed in greater detail below[8]:

Table: Growth Phases of an Organization

Growth Phase	Resulting Crisis	Organizational Needs	Action to Be Taken
Growth through creativity	Crisis of leadership	More formalized management practices	Leaders must adapt practices or hire managers to assume this authority
Growth through direction	Crisis of autonomy	Lower level managers need more authority	Leaders must delegate authority
Growth through delegation	Crisis of control	Employees need autonomy to do jobs while leaders need to feel in control	Leaders must develop a system of checks and balances
Growth through coordination	Crisis of bureaucracy	Focus groups, planning processes, and staff cause delays in decision-making; innovation suffers.	Management must develop collaborative teams and break down silos.
Growth through collaboration	No formal crisis indicated. However, employees may grow exhausted by teamwork and pressure.		

[8] Source: INC.COM. *Organizational Life Cycle,* http://www.inc.com/encyclopedia/organizational-life-cycle.html

Effective leaders are tuned in to the growth phases of the organization and plan accordingly, typically through the strategic planning process. Understanding where the organization lies in the growth cycle also helps leaders respond appropriately to problems and crises, and to make decisions more efficiently. As organizations progress through the life cycle, it is important for leaders to manage change in order to ensure that management and staff are closely aligned with the strategic vision and objectives, in order for them to be carried out effectively.

Granted, not all organizations are able to survive the growth phase in its entirety. Some may collapse due to an inability to respond to changes and demands. Others may simply be acquired by another company and therefore lose their ability to operate autonomously. If an organization does successfully make it through the growth phases, they will reach a point of maturity and eventually decline.

Maturity and Decline

An organization has reached maturity once it has enough resources in order to plan for the future, and has formalized policies and procedures as well as a solid infrastructure in which it operates. In this stage of the organizational life cycle, it is typical for organizations to become bureaucratic, making it more difficult to make decisions or change direction quickly. This characteristic can be detrimental to the organization if its competition or industry evolves at a rapid pace (e.g., developing new products and services).

On the other hand, an organization in the maturity phase also experiences a sense of stability. Having developed departments for functions, as well as formalized procedures, makes it easier to hire and train staff. Additionally, mature organizations also have the financial resources and planning necessary to pay their employees competitively. The phase of maturity may last for several years or decades as long as the organization is able to respond to crises and changes in the environment.

Once an organization has reached a level of high inefficiency and bureaucracy, it will begin to decline. The organization's products or services may be outdated, and sales may decline, due to a lack of innovation. Leadership may respond by reducing the workforce, closing facilities, or finding other cost-cutting measures that reduce redundancy. In order to revive the organization, leaders must find a way to innovate through the development of new or refined products or services that meet the demands of the marketplace. Otherwise, the organization may fail and cease to exist, or it may be acquired by a larger organization in a growth phase.

The Strategic Planning Process

In order to respond to changes in the marketplace and continue to grow, organizations periodically undergo strategic planning, which is a process of defining the overall purpose and desired results of the organization, as well as outlining how those results will be achieved. In other words, through strategic planning, an organization determines where it is going over the next year (or more), how it will get there, and how it will measure its success. Strategic planning focuses on the organization as a whole rather than a particular product or service. The process, which is often done on a periodic basis, answers the following questions about the organization:

1. Where are we now?
2. Where do we want to be in _____ years?
3. How will we get there?
4. How will we know when we are there?

There is a variety of approaches to strategic planning. Depending on the size, organizational leadership, maturity level, and culture, strategic planning may be achieved through any techniques that match the unique needs of the organization[9].

- *Goals-based planning* - focuses on the organizational mission, vision, and values. Goals are set to work toward the mission, and from there determine steps needed to achieve the goals.

- *Issues-based planning* - focuses on issues facing the organization and determines steps to address those issues.

- *Organic planning* - focuses common vision and values, and identifying best practices and methodologies in the organization. The stakeholders focus on what is already working rather than fixing problems.

Regardless of the method, strategic plans are typically created for a period of one year or more. Some plans may be in-depth, with step-by-step action plans, while others may be high-level with no specific steps. In general, though, the strategic planning process will have the following elements:

---

[9] Source: http://managementhelp.org/strategicplanning/index.htm#anchor1234

1. *Planning the process.* Leaders decide on process, participants, and time frame. Pre-planning reduces errors in the planning process and achieves commitment from leaders.

2. *Study the environment,* using tools such as statistical models, SWOT analysis, PEST analysis, and Porter's five forces to determine the organization's present state.

3. *Formulate a strategy.* Develop the organization's mission, vision, values, goals, and objectives. Focus on the future and the direction or destination.

4. *Implement the strategy.* Articulate goals, develop budgets, create action plans, and execute plans.

5. *Evaluate the strategy.* Evaluate the strategy periodically and make adjustments.

Words to Know

- **Statistical models:** Use relevant data to show trends that affect the organization.
- **SWOT analysis:** examines the internal strengths and weaknesses, as well as external opportunities and threats, of the organization.
- **PEST analysis:** *examines external factors (political, economic, social, and technological) as they apply to an organization.*
- **Porter's 5 Forces:** Named after Michael E. Porter, analyzes 5 competitive forces that shape every industry (competition, potential of new entrants, power of suppliers, power of customers, and threat of substitute products), and helps determine an industry's weaknesses and strengths.

The formal strategic plan, however, is not as important as the process itself, as well as the execution of the plan. There are many benefits an organization can find through the strategic planning process as seen in the graphic below.

The Strategic Planning Process

Creates sense of purpose	Sets goals	Enhances communication with staff	Keeps staff involved	Allocates resources appropriately	Creates accountability	Builds consensus

Having stakeholders unite to take time and articulate the future of the organization is a healthy process that will keep the organization adaptable to change and viable in the marketplace. Leveraging the existing organizational hierarchy to execute the plan, and reviewing progress periodically, are keys to a successful implementation of the strategic plan.

Mission, Vision, and Values

During the strategic planning process, an organization typically reviews its mission, vision, and values statements. If the organization has not already created these, or is undergoing the process for the first time, it typically will develop these statements as part of the process. Once these statements are formalized, the organization's goals are developed to support them.

Words to Know

- **Mission statement:** A statement that defines why an organization exists and what its purpose is. At a minimum, the statement should explain who the organization serves (customers), what products or services it offers, and where it offers them.
- **Vision statement:** A statement that explains the aspirations of the organization. It describes the ideal conditions the organization hopes to achieve.
- **Core values:** A description of commonly held values which guide the perspective of the organization and its actions.

Sources:
http://www.entrepreneur.com/encyclopedia/mission-statement
http://ctb.ku.edu/en/table-of-contents/structure/strategic-planning/vision-mission-statements/main
http://smallbusiness.chron.com/organizational-value-statement-23848.html

---

It is important for organizations to develop these statements because it can help the stakeholders focus on what is important. During the strategic planning process, and throughout the year, having these statements can help maintain focus and remind employees what is important as they conduct their day-to-day jobs.

Developing Goals

Once the mission, vision, and values have been developed (or refined), goals are developed to describe how the organization will achieve its mission and vision. Goals should be SMART:

- *Specific* - having enough description to guide action plans
- *Measurable* - have a method for knowing if the goal is met

- *Action-oriented* - describe the actions that will be taken
- *Realistic* - must be achievable
- *Time-based* - include a timeframe for completion

Implementing the Strategic Plan

Once the strategic plan has been developed, organizational leaders will consult with department heads, management, and other key employees to begin the implementation process. This process includes the development of tactical goals and action plans, which can be specific to departments, work groups, or even certain individuals in the organization. The tactical goals and action plans should tie directly to the more broadly stated strategic plan and should be SMART.

After the goals and action plans are developed, leadership and management will address budgetary issues and resources needed to achieve the strategic plan. The organization may decide it needs additional personnel, new technology, or external assistance. Those who are involved in the budgeting process will make recommendations on what cash and resources are needed, and leadership will determine whether the recommendation will support the strategic plan.

Evaluating the Strategic Plan

Strategic planning does not end with the development of that plan. Rather, it is a continual process that occurs throughout the year or years. As the organization implements its plan, it should periodically evaluate whether it is on track to achieve the strategic goals. This would include evaluating the tactical goals and action plans, as well. If the organization's leaders find that the organization is not on track, they may decide to revise the action plan or tactical goals, or re-evaluate the strategic plan itself. Sometimes, internal or external factors may cause an organization to change course. Those organizations that are able to adapt accordingly to their environment are likely to succeed.

The Role of HR in Strategic Planning

Human resource leaders have an important role in the strategic planning process. During it, each department or business unit, including HR, develops its own goals and action plans that align with the overarching goals of the organization. The strategic HR plan addresses the same questions used during the larger strategic planning process. It should answer where the function is now, where it is heading (with the organization), how the team will get there, and how they will know that they are there. As with any strategic plan, the strategic HR plan will differ from organization to organization. However, there are some common elements, as outlined in the following table

Table: Components of a Human Capital Plan[10]

Component	Explanation
Strategic direction	The strategic direction requires knowledge about the organization's strategic plans, budgetary constraints, internal and external forces affecting human capital, makeup of the current workforce, and customer and stakeholder expectations, challenges, and needs. It is important to develop a vision of the kind of future workforce needed. This will help frame the desired state of human capital for the organization to achieve its strategic plan.
Human capital goals	Human capital goals are related to the organization's talent (employees), performance management, and leadership. Goals can involve the hiring, training, and allocation of employees to achieve certain goals or objectives in the overarching strategic plan.
Strategies for accomplishing goals	The strategies (or objectives) specifically describe more how the goals will be achieved. When developing objectives, it is consideration should be given to the availability and capabilities of human capital.
Implementation plan	The implementation plan describes the actions needed to carry out the goals and objectives. Implementation plans include the following components: • A description of each task necessary to carry out the objectives • Who is responsible for each task • Resources required (e.g., human, financial) • Timeframes (e.g., milestones, deadlines)

---

[10] Source: http://www.opm.gov/policy-data-oversight/human-capital-management/reference-materials/strategic-alignment/keycomponents.pdf

Communications plan	The communications plan describes how key stakeholders in the organization will stay informed about the progress of the strategic plan, as well as actions they need to take. It is important to communicate regularly with all stakeholders to ensure that the plan is well understood and that feedback is received. The communications plan is closely tied with the implementation plan and is often a subset of it.
Accountability system	The accountability system describes how progress in executing the strategy or objective will be measured and tracked. People and teams identified in the implementation plan are those who are held accountable. Specific targets can be identified by describing the level of performance or rate of improvement needed for each part of the implementation plan. Establishing metrics can provide essential direction to those involved in executing the objectives, and can give the organization insight into the progress of implementing the plan.

Once human resources leadership establishes a human capital management plan, they will then develop a budget to support the implementation of this plan. Depending on alignment of the organization's finances, the human resources departmental budget may include these costs:

- Employee compensation (salaries, bonuses, and benefits)
- Payroll taxes
- Equipment and supplies
- Training and development fees
- Travel
- Outsourced services (e.g., payroll, benefits administration, HRIS)

HR may also lead the development of budgetary items that are then allocated to other departments or verticals in the organization. These costs may include:

- Recruitment fees
- Training and development fees
- Raises
- Employee incentives or awards
- Temporary staff

As with any function in the organization, it is important for the human resources function to closely align with the goals of the organization. This includes aligning HR resources and services. In some cases, it may be more cost-effective to outsource functions or repurpose HR positions to carry out new or different tasks. Processes can be streamlined, too, so that HR personnel can focus their efforts on tasks that are more impactful to the organization.

Managing Organizational Change

As a result of the strategic planning process, an organization may decide that it needs to restructure itself in order to achieve its goals and remain competitive and viable in the marketplace. Organizational leadership may decide to explore or implement any of the following structural changes[11].

- *Restructuring or re-engineering* - Examine processes for redundancy in the entire organization or in certain departments or teams. Simplify operations in order to improve efficiency and reduce costs.

- *Expansion in force* - Grow teams through the creation of new positions and hiring additional personnel. This can lead to a culture clash between veteran employees and newcomers. It will require resources to train the new employees and acclimate them to the new environment.

- *Reduction in force* - Also called downsizing; decrease personnel expense by eliminating positions or departments. This often creates anxiety for remaining employees who must take on the extra workload while feeling uncertain about their own jobs.

- *Mergers and acquisitions* - Involves combining two or more entities. Mergers are the result of two companies joining to leverage both of their assets while forming a new, stronger corporate identity. Acquisitions involve a larger company purchasing another company and integrating it into the existing culture and operations.

- *Divestiture* - Involves a company's product line, service, or business unit being spun off or sold. Typically, the existing team involved in the divestiture remains intact.

- *Outsourcing* - Use external service providers to handle certain business functions, such as accounting, payroll, or IT.

---

[11] Sources:http://www.orgchart.net/wiki/HR_in_Mergers_and_Acquisitions

[11] http://www.orgchart.net/wiki/Reorganization

[11] http://www.orgchart.net/wiki/Workforce_Planning

- *Offshoring* - Move certain jobs or functions to other countries where labor is cheaper, in order to achieve cost savings. This has other implications, such as a loss of jobs elsewhere, cultural barriers, and time zone differences.

Employees are all affected by organizational change in some way. In some cases, it may mean an addition or change in responsibilities. For others, it may mean a loss of their job (or a fear of loss). HR professionals can help manage organizational change by putting in place programs and communications to help employees understand the changes, manage their emotions, and adapt to the restructuring. It is important for the organization to communicate regularly with employees to keep them apprised about the changes, let them know how they are impacted, and be truthful about the facts. If the organization is not truthful, or employees perceive that that information is being withheld from them, it risks losing longer-term employees who might otherwise stay. This can have a long-term negative impact on the organization in terms of a loss of productivity and a loss of historical knowledge.

Corporate governance refers to the set of systems, principles and processes that guide everything a company does, including the relationships between its stakeholders (i.e., board of directors, management, and shareholders). Managing ethics in the workplace holds tremendous benefit for stakeholders, and it greatly affects other key constituents including customers, employees, and the public. In other words, when stakeholders make decisions for the organization, it affects how the employees act and how the public responds.

Corporate governance is based on principles such as transparency, integrity, fairness, compliance, accountability, and responsibility. To achieve these qualities, an organization typically has an active, independent board of directors that serves to oversee the organization and represents the shareholders' interests. The board of directors typically includes inside directors (those who work for the organization) and outside directors (those who do not have an employment relationship with the organization). The board is typically elected by the shareholders (who are owners of the corporation). Management, including executives, are employees of the organization and oversee the day-to-day operations of the organization.

A corporation, while a legal entity, cannot make a decision for itself. Instead, the board of directors and management must make decisions for the organization. These stakeholders have a fiduciary responsibility to the organization, meaning that they should make decisions that are in the best interests of stakeholders and the organization's survival, rather than their own personal interests. Of course, this does not always happen in the real world. In response to corporate scandals in the early 2000's by Enron and WorldCom, the Sarbanes-Oxley Act was enacted in 2002 to ensure that stakeholders in public corporations appropriately maintain and uphold their fiduciary responsibilities.

The Sarbanes Oxley Act of 2002[12]

SOX was enacted to make unethical practices illegal in public corporations and provide penalties for violations. Among its provisions include the following:

1. The Public Company Accounting Oversight Board was developed to require all public accounting firms to register with the board, who could audit the company's records for compliance.

---

[12] Sources: http://gbr.pepperdine.edu/2010/08/reforming-corporate-america/

[12]http://en.wikipedia.org/wiki/Sarbanes%E2%80%93Oxley_Act

2. Standards were established to maintain the independent nature of auditors. Results of audits (including recommendations) are now provided directly to the audit committee of the organization's board of directors.

3. Standards for corporate responsibility were established, and the organization's chief executive is held accountable for the accuracy of filings with the Securities and Exchange Commission.

4. CEO's and CFO's are required to forfeit bonuses or gains through shares of stock for a one-year period when the organization files a restatement of financial reports with the SEC due to misconduct.

5. Insider trading of stock is prohibited during pension fund blackout periods.

6. CFO's must satisfy certain ethical requirements.

7. Management officials who commit fraud or obstruct justice face criminal penalties.

8. Whistleblowers who report misconduct they reasonably believe to violate SEC regulations or federal laws are protected.

Corporate Ethics

A commitment to doing the right thing trickles down from the highest levels of an organization. When the organization's directors, officers, and managers show their commitment to behaving ethically, employees are prone to follow their example. Many organizations, whether or not they are subject to SOX compliance, often demonstrate their commitment to corporate responsibility by developing organization-wide ethics statements, values statements, and codes of conduct.

Words to Know

- **Code of ethics** – describes the ideal standards the organization wants to achieve when conducting business
- **Code of conduct** – describes the behaviors an organization expects from its employees, as well as disciplinary action for violations

Source:
http://en.wikipedia.org/wiki/Ethical_code#Code_of_ethics_or_a_code_of_conduct.3F_.28corporate_or_business_ethics.29

Within the code of conduct, the organization should indicate how conflicts of interest, insider information, and gifts should be handled. Conflicts of interest arise when an employee may personally benefit from the action of the organization. Typically, the employee is required, at minimum, to disclose potential conflicts of interest, and management will identify ways to avoid or mitigate the conflict. Gifts from vendors or clients to an employee in the organization are a type of conflict of interest identified in such a policy. Insider information can lead to a conflict of interest when the employee has access to information that the general public does not have. Using insider information to make decisions on the purchase or sale of stock is prohibited by law and carries criminal and civil penalties.

Whistleblower Protection

Under the Sarbanes Oxley Act, violations of securities laws or a breach of fiduciary duty must be reported to the chief legal officer or CEO of the organization. An organization's legal team (in house or external counsel) must also report these violations to the organization's board of directors audit committee. SOX also provides protections for people who, in good faith, report suspected or witnessed wrongdoing. These people are called whistleblowers, which include people who report violations, people who assist those reporting violations, as well as people who assist in an investigation. Whistleblower protections are regulated by the Department of Labor and the Occupational Safety and Health Administration (OSHA). Under OSHA regulations, in particular, an employer is prohibited from taking adverse action against whistleblowers, including termination of employment, reducing pay, discipline, intimidation, coercion, or any other type of retaliation. Publicly traded companies are required by SOX to establish confidential whistleblower complaints, and maintain those records according to the rules established in the law. Organizations that are not publicly traded (and therefore not subject to SOX) may elect, at their own will, to establish whistleblower policies and procedures in order to maintain an ethical workplace[13].

Ethics Officers

Organizations committed to maintaining ethical standards often choose a key person to serve as an ethics officer. The ethics officer may be a person at the executive level, the company's internal legal counsel, or the highest-ranking human resources professional. Ethics officers advise all employees in the organization on their obligations to maintain an ethical workplace.

---

[13] Source: http://www.whistleblowers.org/index.php?option=com_content&task=view&id=27

They inform employees about what is right to do, and what is not acceptable conduct. They oversee the training of all employees on ethical matters, and develop policies to maintain compliance with SOX (as applicable) and consistency with corporate values and ethics. Ethics officers also provide advice to other organizational leaders when ethical issues arise.

Organizational Design & Development

Organizational design is the alignment of people, processes, compensation, and metrics with the strategy of the organization. It also provides the framework through which an organization can embody its core values as specified in its vision statement[14]. The design reflects the organization's need to respond to changes (internal and external), integrate new people, technologies, and processes, encourage collaboration and offer flexibility. An organization can be organized in different ways, depending on its objectives. Leaders and managers must make decisions about how to group people together to perform their work effectively.

There are five common approaches to organizational design that help decision makers with grouping people (i.e., positions) together in the organization[15].

- *Functional structure* groups positions into departments or units based on similar tasks, expertise, skills, and resources. Examples of groups within a function structure are accounting/finance, human resources, information technology, and marketing.

- *Divisional structure* groups business units according to a type of output. For example, units may be aligned with specific geographic locales, products, or clients.

- *Matrix structure* is a hybrid of functional and divisional structure. People work in teams that integrate disparate expertise. Employees working in a matrix structure belong to both a functional and a divisional group (e.g., project team or product team).

- *Team structure* integrates separate functions into a group based on a particular goal or objective. Teams serve to break down organizational silos instead foster collaboration, cooperation, problem solving, and relationship building among various functions.

- *Network structure* involves external entities performing certain functions on a temporary or contractual basis. Work is assigned, for example, to a contractor for a period of time in order to achieve a certain goal.

Organizational structures evolve over time as the organization grows, its environment changes, or other circumstances make it necessary for the organization to survive. Part of the strategic planning process is to identify ways to maintain a sound structure that keeps the organization positioned to achieve the organization's goals and objectives. In other words, the structure of the organization should support what the organization hopes to achieve. Otherwise, the organization will be at a disadvantage and may risk losing its competitiveness.

---

[14] Source: http://en.wikipedia.org/wiki/Organizational_architecture#Design

[15] Source: http://en.wikipedia.org/wiki/Organizational_structure

41

Centralized vs. Decentralized Decision Making

In addition to the physical structure of the organization, it is important to consider the structure of decision-making. Decisions are constantly made in an organization: who to hire, what products or services to offer, where to operate, what clients to target and more. Decision making in an organization can be either centralized or decentralized.

Centralized organizational structures rely on one individual (or group of executives) to make decisions and provide direction for the organization. Smaller organizations often use this structure because the owner is responsible for the company's business operations. As a benefit, centralized organizations often experience quick, efficient decision-making, as opposed to flat organizations that require collaboration. Business owners typically set the company's mission, vision, goals, and objectives, which managers are expected to support and execute. However, centralized organizations can become bureaucratic as they grow, due to the number of management layers stretching to the owner. Keeping decision-making centralized can require more time to accomplish tasks, which results in slower operations and lower productivity.

Decentralized organizational structures, on the other hand, often have several individuals responsible for making decisions for running the organization. Decentralized organizations rely on a team environment at different level of the business, in order to make decisions. (Individuals may have some autonomy to make business decisions, but generally must be aligned with the vision of the larger group). Decentralized organizations typically employ individuals with a variety of knowledge and skills for running various business operations, ensuring that the company is positioned to handle various types of business situations. However, decentralized organizations can struggle with an inability to reach consensus due to multiple opinions of decision makers. This can harm the organization's ability to move forward with carrying out its objectives, and it can harm productivity.

There is no right or wrong decision-making structure for an organization to adopt. Organizational leadership should carefully consider their work styles, personalities, goals, vision, and overall environment when deciding upon the right structure for the organization. Small organizations typically adopt centralized decision-making structures because owners often remain at the forefront of business operations. Larger organizations often utilize a more decentralized structure because they have several divisions or departments. Additionally, business leaders may need to consider changing the organizational structure depending on the growth of the business as well as its overall strategy[16].

---

[16] http://smallbusiness.chron.com/centralized-vs-decentralized-organizational-structure-2785.html

Organizing Work Performed in Organizations

Regardless of how they are structured, organizations are all groups of people who work together toward a common goal. To efficiently accomplish their goals, organizations typically divide work into manageable parts, particularly when there are many different tasks to perform. They also coordinate the work that employees do to ensure that everyone is working interdependently toward the same objectives.

Definition of Division of Labor

Division of labor refers to the distribution of work into separate jobs that are performed by different people. Division of labor leads to job specialization, because each job will eventually have a narrower subset of the tasks to achieve the company's goals and objectives. As companies grow over time, horizontal division of labor (i.e., many people doing similar jobs) is usually accompanied by a vertical division of labor (i.e., managers and supervisors overseeing jobs performed). Job specialization also increases work efficiency. Workers can master smaller tasks quickly, and less time is wasted changing from one task to another. Training costs are also reduced because employees require fewer skills to accomplish the assigned work. Finally, job specialization makes it easier to recruit and hire people that are suited for the jobs[17].

How Work Activities Are Coordinated

An organization's ability to divide work among employees depends on how well those people can collaborate and work with one another. Otherwise, productivity suffers due to the misallocation of tasks or resources, or duplication of effort. Coordination tends to become more challenging as jobs become more specialized. Therefore, companies typically specialize jobs up to a point in which it is feasible to coordinate the people in those jobs. Every organization uses one or more of the following mechanisms to coordinate work: informal communication, formal hierarchy, and standardization[18].

- *Informal Communication* - includes sharing information with other employees via face-to-face interaction, email, and conference calls. Team meetings are a common source of informal communication, where tactical matters are discussed and work is coordinated at a more specific level.

---

[17] Source: http://en.wikipedia.org/wiki/Division_of_labour

[18] Source: http://www.provenmodels.com/17/six-coordination-mechanisms/henry-mintzberg

- *Hierarchy/Supervision* - gives authority to individuals at certain levels of the organization, who then direct work processes and allocate resources. This is also known as the chain of command.

- *Standardization* - involves the development of routine processes, measured outputs, and required training or competencies.

Span of Control

Span of control refers to the number of direct reports a manager has. A small number of direct reports for each manager will create a **narrow span** of control and a lengthy hierarchical structure, also known as a **tall organization**. On the other hand, a **wide span** of control means a larger number of direct reports for each manager, creating a **flat organization**. Although there likely is no perfect ratio of direct reports to a given manager, span of control is helpful in understanding organizational design and behaviors[19]. Therefore, many factors will need to be evaluated before determining the best ratio within an organization.

- *Organizational size* - Due to costs, large organizations tend to have a narrow span of control, while smaller organizations typically have a wider span of control.

- *Skills required for jobs* - Routine tasks involving fewer skills will require less supervision, allowing a wider span of control. Complex tasks may need a narrower span of control, where supervisors can provide more individualized attention.

- *Organizational culture* - Flexible workplaces typically have a wider span of control because the organization provides a more autonomous environment in which employees need little supervision.

- *Workload of managers* - Managers need to be effective with the number of direct reports they have. They should be able to plan departmental activities, train staff, and manage performance while being accountable for their own individual responsibilities.

Spans of control can be purposefully widened by giving workers more autonomy and holding them accountable to manage themselves. They can also be widened by standardizing the work processes of junior employees to avoid costly mistakes. As the span of control gets larger in an organization, it greatly increases the number of relationships among managers.

---

[19] Source: http://www.shrm.org/TemplatesTools/hrqa/Pages/Whatfactorsshoulddeterminehowmanydirectreportsamanagerhas.aspx

Leadership

Researches have studied leadership extensively. Leadership takes many different forms, and different approaches are appropriate for different circumstances. Since the early 20th century, several categories of leadership theories have developed: trait theories, behavioral theories, contingency theories, and power/influence theories[20].

Leadership Theories

Trait Theories

Trait theories maintain that effective leaders share a number of common traits, beliefs, and thought processes. Early trait theorists believed that that leadership is an innate quality that a person either does or does not have. Over time, this theory has evolved to an understanding that people can develop leadership qualities within themselves and help others develop. Now, trait theories help people to identify traits and qualities (such as integrity, charisma, empathy, assertiveness, and problem-solving skills) that are helpful when leading others. However, there is no specific combination of traits that makes an ideal leader.

Behavioral Theories

Behavioral theories focus on how leaders act toward others. In the 1930s, Kurt Lewin (known as the father of modern social psychology[21]) developed a leadership framework based on a leader's behavior. He argued that three styles of leadership exist[22]:

1. *Autocratic* leaders make decisions with little or no input from their subordinates. They dictate what needs to be done and how it needs to be done. This style of leadership is best applied when quick decisions are needed, but input is not.

2. *Democratic* leaders offer guidance to the team but allow team members to provide input before making a decision. This style is effective when team agreement matters, but it can be challenging when team members have conflicting perspectives and ideas.

---

[20] Source: http://www.mindtools.com/pages/article/leadership-theories.htm

[21] Source: http://psychology.about.com/od/profilesofmajorthinkers/p/bio_lewin.htm

[22] Source: http://psychology.about.com/od/leadership/a/leadstyles.htm

3. *Laissez-faire* leaders allow team members to make many of the decisions on their own. This approach works well when the team is skilled, motivated, and doesn't need close supervision. Oversight is still required to ensure that the team stays on track.

No behavioral style is perfect. Good managers are able to use a combination of these three styles as appropriate for each situation they encounter. They should be adaptable based on the needs of their teams and the organization.

Contingency Theories

Because researchers agree there is no one correct type of leader, and that different leadership styles can be used effectively in different situations, contingency theories argue which style is best in which circumstance. The Hersey-Blanchard Situational Leadership Theory, for example, links leadership style with the maturity of individual members of the leader's team. Other contingency-based models include House's Path-Goal Theory, which says that leadership should depend on the team members' needs, the task that they're doing, and the environment that they're working in.

Power and Influence Theories

Power and influence theories are based on the different ways that leaders leverage their power and influence to get things done. French and Raven's Five Forms of Power[23] outlines three types of positional power – legitimate, reward, and coercive – and two sources of personal power – expert and referent (charisma). The model suggests that using personal power is more effective, specifically expert power (becoming an expert at what you do).

Another leadership style, transactional leadership, assumes that people are motivated by rewards for things they do. Therefore, this approach focuses on designing tasks and reward structures. The "transaction" involves the organization paying team members in exchange for their completion of a task or job. The leader will "punish" team members whose work does not meet an appropriate standard. This approach is used in most organizations to get things done, despite the fact that it does not focus on the "people" aspect of leadership, such as developing relationships.

---

[23] Source: http://changingminds.org/explanations/power/french_and_raven.htm

Other Leadership Styles

There are other leadership styles that do not fit within the other frameworks previously mentioned, but are still relevant in the workplace.

Bureaucratic Leadership

Bureaucratic leaders follow rules closely, and expect the same of their team members. This style is effective when working in dangerous conditions (e.g., operating heavy machinery, working with hazardous substances), when working directly with money, or when performing routine tasks. This style is much less effective in teams that require flexibility, creativity, or innovation.

Charismatic Leadership

A charismatic leadership style seeks to inspire and motivate team members. Leaders who rely on charisma often focus on themselves and their own ambitions, however, and they may not want to make an impact on the organization as a whole. Charismatic leaders might have an air of infallibility, which can have damaging effects on the organization if significant, inappropriate decisions are made.

Servant Leadership

A "servant leader" is someone who leads by meeting the needs of the team. These individuals often lead by example, and have high integrity and show great generosity. This approach can foster a positive culture and high morale on the team. Servant leadership requires time and dedication and may not be compatible with the more authoritarian, rigid types of leadership.

Transformational Leadership

Transformational leaders inspire their team members because they expect the best from everyone, and they hold themselves accountable for their actions. They set clear goals, and they have good conflict-resolution skills. This leads to high productivity and engagement.

According to researcher Bernard M. Bass, they gain trust, respect, and admiration from others[24].

As shown by these many frameworks and styles, leadership is not a "one size fits all" concept; instead, leaders must adapt their approach to fit a particular situation. It is important for leaders to develop a thorough understanding of the various leadership frameworks and styles, so that they can be flexible.

---

[24] Source: http://psychology.about.com/od/leadership/a/transformational.htm

Human resource management describes the activities involved with managing an organization's employees, also known as its human capital. HR professionals oversee the "people" aspects of an organization including compensation and benefits, training and development, recruitment and hiring, strategic management, and other functions. The objective of HR departments, essentially, is to recruit, retain, and motivate the best employees for the organization. To do so, they find ways to keep the company competitive in terms of its compensation, benefits, learning opportunities, career advancement, work/life balance, and other aspects that are important to employees. At the same time, HR plays the role of business partner to the organization as it finds ways to allocate staff appropriately, maintain regulatory compliance, and help prevent risk. Having people needs aligned with business needs is essential to the organization's viability and attractiveness in the marketplace.

There are several HR functions or areas of expertise, including recruitment, safety, employee relations, compensation & benefits, and compliance[25]. HR practitioners may perform a combination of these or may specialize in one or a few. Some small businesses without a dedicated HR professional outsource these functions or join a professional employer organization in order to obtain the same benefits of an internal HR team.

Recruitment

Talent acquisition, or recruitment, in a human resources organization can be performed by internal recruiters, employment specialists, or HR generalists. As part of the overall recruitment process, they advertise and post jobs, source resumes, screen candidates, conduct first round interviews, and coordinate with the hiring manager (or team). In larger organizations, the success of recruiters is measured by the time to fill job openings (called requisitions) as well as the number of positions they fill. Recruitment can also be performed by external agencies or headhunters, who are not employed by the organization.

Safety

Workplace safety is essential, and particular attention to safety issues is needed when workers operate heavy machinery, are exposed to chemicals or harmful substances, or work in otherwise dangerous places or situations. Employee safety is mandated through the federal

---

[25] Source: http://smallbusiness.chron.com/six-main-functions-human-resource-department-60693.html

Occupational Safety and Health Act of 1970. HR often facilitates or oversees safety training and maintains federally mandated logs for workplace injuries and fatalities that are reported to the government. HR also manages workers' compensation issues for on-the-job injuries.

Employee Relations

Employee relations involves strengthening the employer-employee relationship through measuring job satisfaction, maintaining employee engagement, and resolving workplace conflicts or grievances. Employee relations also involves coaching employees and managers to handle difficult situations, investigating sexual harassment and discrimination claims, placing employees on performance improvement plans, and terminating employees. In a unionized work environment, labor relations functions may include responding to union organizing campaigns, negotiating collective bargaining agreements, and interpreting union contracts. The employee and labor relations functions of HR may be combined and handled by one specialist or be entirely separate functions managed by two HR specialists with specific expertise in each area.

Compensation and Benefits

Like employee and labor relations, the compensation and benefits functions of HR often can be handled by one HR specialist with dual expertise. On the compensation side, HR functions include setting compensation and evaluating competitive pay practices. A comp and benefits specialist also may negotiate group health coverage rates with insurers and coordinate with the retirement savings fund administrator. Payroll can be a component of the compensation and benefits section of HR, but in many cases, employers outsource such administrative functions.

Compliance

Compliance with local, state, and federal labor laws is an essential HR function. Noncompliance can result in litigation and governmental complaints based on unfair employment practices, unsafe working conditions, fines from the government, and overall dissatisfaction among employees. HR staff must be aware of federal, state, and local employment laws such as Fair Labor Standards Act, Title VII of the Civil Rights Act, the National Labor Relations Act, the Family and Medical Leave Act, and many more. To comply with these laws and maintain fairness in the organization, HR professionals help develop company policies and procedure manuals.

Training and Development

Employers must provide employees with the training and tools necessary for their success. New employees should receive an orientation to help them transition to the new organization and receive adequate training. Many HR departments also coordinate leadership training and ongoing professional development activities. Depending on the organization's financial resources, programs such as tuition assistance programs for college or advanced degrees often are offered within the training and development area.

HR Information Systems (HRIS)

HRIS professionals maintain all personnel (and sometimes payroll) records, including employee names, addresses, emergency contacts, job and pay information, performance ratings, leaves of absence, benefit elections, and more. They also provide reports to leaders and managers to support personnel decisions, or monitor certain employee metrics such as turnover. The HRIS function may be handled by a particular HRIS specialist, or it may be handled by a departmental assistant, HR generalist, or other type of specialist.

HR Generalist vs. Specialist

HR professionals typically fall within one of two categories: generalist or specialist. HR generalists, also commonly called HR managers or HR business partners, have a broad range of responsibilities in one or more of the functional areas of human resources. Larger organizations typically have HR specialists with technical knowledge and skills in specific areas. There are typically different levels of generalists and specialists in an organization, depending on its size, budget, and other needs. Examples of specialist job titles can be found in the table below.

Table: Functional Areas of HR & Related Job Titles

Functional Area	Job Title Examples
Recruiting	Recruiter Recruiting Assistant/Coordinator Talent Acquisition Specialist Staffing Manager

Training & Organizational Development	Learning & Organizational Development Manager Organizational Development Specialist
Compensation & Benefits	Compensation Analyst Benefits Specialist Total Rewards Manager
Employee & Labor Relations	Performance Manager Specialist Employee Relations Manager Labor Relations Manager
Safety	Risk Management Specialist Workers Compensation Specialist
HR Information Systems	HRIS Administrator HRIS Manager

The HR Business Partner Model

More recently, the tactical HR generalist role has transformed into a business partner, with an aim to collaborate with senior leadership and help them develop and execute "people" strategies. Yet, the administrative and tactical aspects of HR remain necessary for business operations. In order to be influential in the organization, HR business partners need to position themselves as strategic advisors, champions for change, and operations managers.

Developing a deep understanding of the organization, its operations, and its external environment is essential for any HR business partner to become a strategic advisor to senior management. They must align themselves closely with the values of the organization and the visions of the leaders in order to be seen as valuable partners. To do this they must:

- Learn all they can about the business -- its operations, financials, and strategy
- Influence the strategic agenda by building relationships at key levels in the organization
- Earn leaders' trust so that HR can contribute to business results
- Be able to prioritize processes that will deliver the most benefits
- Develop credibility through competence, honesty, and high standards
- Champion HR solutions that will add to the bottom line today and for future needs
- Act as a catalyst for continued business performance

As a business partner, HR practitioners share in responsibility for the success of the business by executing HR strategies that lead to tangible results. HR business partners should be able to quantify HR's contribution to business performance and staff effectiveness in business operations. HR business partners can help align activities with the right people with the right skills, design meaningful career paths to motivate employees, actively manage talent, design staffing and succession plans and foster an open work environment where ideas are shared[26].

Policies and Procedures

As organizations grow, they need to develop policies and procedures to maintain consistency throughout the organization, convey important information to employees, and stay compliant with federal and state laws. Having clearly communicated human resources policies and procedures provides consistency in message and administration of the policies of the organization. Documented policies can also protect the organization in the event of a lawsuit or complaint. Federal laws, such as the Civil Rights Act of 1964, mandate that all employees should be treated equally, and HR policies and procedures can help the organization formalize the way the organization achieves that objective.

One goal of policies should be to support managers in handling personnel issues. A supervisor who reads and understands the written policies of the organization can answer employee questions and grievances and handle minor disciplinary issues without always involving the human resources department. For example, if two employees in different departments are consistently late or not meeting performance standards, having set policies that address how to handle these situations will provide the guidance that managers need to treat employees fairly. If an employee questions the supervisor's handling of an employment issue, the supervisor can reference the HR policies, helping the supervisor maintain authority while remaining unbiased.

Policies and procedures help employees, too. By providing handbooks to employees, organizations can empower employees to find information on their own and understand their responsibilities. An employee with questions on work hours, paychecks, dress code, paid time off, harassment, or other employment related issues can find answers on their own. In addition, complete policies can also provide the employee with guidance on who to contact with concerns about their employment or specific issues. Ultimately, policies provide protection to the organization. In the event of litigation or a complaint regarding an employment action, the manual can serve as an example of how the organization administers policies consistently and fairly. Human resource professionals should reference the policies when responding to

---

[26] Source: http://www.shrm.org/Communities/StudentPrograms/Pages/careersinHRM.aspx

questions and coach supervisors on the appropriate methods or procedures to document employee disciplinary problems. Policies and procedures should be reviewed periodically and updated to reflect changes in federal and state laws relating to employees, as well as changes in the work environment or organizational structure.

Technology and Management Systems

The Human Resource Information System (HRIS) is a type of HR management system or electronic platform for data entry, tracking, and reporting human resources data. The system maintains important static information about employees such as their addresses, social security numbers, tax withholding information, job and pay information, and benefit elections. The HRIS can typically produce static reports such as employee lists, as well as analytical reports such as turnover, headcount, and other information useful for planning purposes. HRIS vendors package their systems with various capabilities, and some are more robust than others. Typically, a HRIS will provide the organization with:

- The ability to manage all employee information and records
- The ability to track applicants.
- Reporting capabilities on HR metrics
- The ability to post HR documents such as employee handbooks, procedures, and forms
- Benefits administration
- Integration with payroll or other HR management systems

Graphic: Information Collected in HRIS

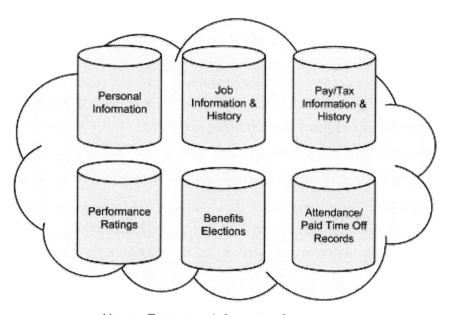

Human Resources Information System

The HRIS should provide information on most data the company needs to track and analyze about applicants, employees, former employees. Some systems allow employees to do their own basic information updates (such as address changes or tax withholdings), as well as benefit enrollments. This frees HR staff to complete strategic functions rather than administrative data entry. Additionally, data recorded can be used to make decisions regarding employment such as merit increases, promotions, and restructuring. Managers can also access information to effectively support the success of their direct reports.

Other HR Management Systems

- *An applicant tracking system (ATS)* is a program that automates the application and recruitment process. An ATS allows job seekers to find and apply for jobs on the company's website through the electronic submission of an application with a resume and cover letter attached. Data is collected from internal applications through the ATS interface, located on the company website, or is sometimes extracted from applicants through job boards. On the employer's side, recruiters can post jobs, search through submitted applications, track candidate progress, and even communicate with applicants through the system. Despite the many capabilities of an ATS, its main function is to provide a central location and database to support the company's recruiting activities. The ATS helps recruiters maintain resumes and applications, and stay compliant with federal and state employment and document retention laws.

- *A learning management system (LMS)* is an application that supports an organization's training and development activities, and provides for the delivery of online training courses, tracking of progress, housing of learning aids, and reporting. Corporate training departments use an LMS to deliver online training, maintain electronic records, and automate employee registration in training programs.

HR Metrics

HR metrics (measurements) can show important trends and information about the organization's people. This information can help leaders make important decisions on how to improve the organization and meet the needs of employees. There are a number of metrics that HR practitioners can track and analyze.

Table: Common HR Metrics

Metric	Calculation
Cost per hire	recruitment costs -- (compensation cost + benefits cost)
Average time to fill a position	sum of days to fill all jobs in a period -- total jobs filled in the period
Absence rate	# days absent in month for all employees -- (average # of employees during a month x # of workdays)
Benefit costs per employee	total cost of employee benefit/program -- total employees
Benefit utilization rate	total number of employees utilizing a benefit -- total number of employees eligible to utilize a benefit
Average Tenure	total service for all active employees -- total number of active employees
Turnover (annual)	# of employees terminating during 12 month period -- average # of employees during the same period
Turnover costs	total costs of separation + recruitment costs + lost productivity + training costs

There are more calculations that organizations can track and measure, depending on your organization's needs. When deciding which metrics to analyze and track, consider these factors:

- What metrics are important to organizational leaders and the strategic plan?
- What data needs to be gathered to calculate these metrics, and from what sources?
- How will the data be analyzed, what against what sources will it be benchmarked?
- How can the analysis be presented for use with will planning, development, and problem-solving?

Mergers and Acquisitions

When a company undergoes a merger or acquisition, the human resources department is a valuable partner in the process. HR helps the organization conduct its due diligence when evaluating a potential merger, plan a strategy for integrating employees of the other company, and manage the change process. Given the complex nature of mergers & acquisitions (M&A's), human resources can provide particular expertise in several areas. [27]

Evaluating Company Culture

Every company has its own unique culture, and when two companies combine into one (through a merger or acquisition), there can be an element of culture shock. When a company is considering an M&A, it should engage its human resources department in evaluating the culture of the other company and analyze how well that company would integrate with the other. Organizational culture affects how employees work; what benefits they receive; how formal or informal the rules are; how people are managed; and what work styles, attitudes, or values the population shares. HR can find out much of this information through the discovery process, in which policies, procedures, communications, and other important documents are confidentially shared and evaluated. If there are significant differences between the two organizations, they should be thoroughly addressed prior to the merger or acquisition.

Identifying Compensation & Benefits Issues

During the due diligence process, the purchasing organization must also make a determination of whether the deal makes financial sense. Part of the financial data includes compensation and benefits. HR should review the compensation structures and benefit plans that the other company offers. It should identify whether the compensation structures and pay levels are compatible with that of the purchasing organization. It should also determine whether there are any issues with the benefit plans, such as a difference in premium costs, coverage levels, or funding of retirement plans (i.e., company match on a 401(k) plan).

---

[27] Source: http://smallbusiness.chron.com/role-human-resources-mergers-acquisitions-23589.html

Managing Change

Change is not easy for most people. When a merger or acquisition occurs, employees may fear for the safety of their jobs, or feel uncertain about the future. HR can help alleviate some of the anxiety by communicating regularly with employees, being responsive to their questions, and being open to feedback. HR should monitor employee morale and identify any challenges, fears, or rumors that arise due to the M&A. HR can help alleviate these roadblocks, dispel rumors, and make the transition smoother. People often fear change, and a merger or acquisition creates uncertainty and change for employees of both companies.

Organizational Design & Development

When one company merges with or acquires another, some functions or jobs may be consolidated due to redundancy. This process may happen quickly, or it may happen over time as the organizations integrate over time. HR plays an active role in restructuring the "new" organization, identifying ways to work more efficiently, and evaluating the impacts of change. HR professionals are responsible for communicating the changes to employees; revising job descriptions; handling difficult situations such as layoffs or resistance to change; training employees on new skills they may need; and finding ways to keep employees feeling motivated.

Main Ideas to Remember

→ Strategic management is the process of creation, research, reassessment, and development. It is important to HR professionals because it affects how HR can add value to the organization through policies, procedures, and programs.

→ All businesses operating in the United States are formally organized into these basic structures: sole proprietorship, partnership, limited liability company, or corporation.

→ There are common functions that can be found within almost every organization: procurement/distribution, development, operations, marketing/sales, and customer service. Core support functions include human resources, accounting/finance, information technology, and facilities.

→ External forces, such as the economy, consumer demand, laws and regulations, technology, and the labor force can greatly affect operations. Being proactive and adapting to these changes accordingly can help an organization remain strong.

→ Like people, organizations have their own life cycles. They are "born" (established), they develop and mature, they decline, and sometimes they "die" (dissolve). The life cycle of a viable organization includes birth, youth, mid-life, and maturity.

→ Through strategic planning, an organization determines its present state, where it is going over the next year (or more), how it will get there, and how it will measure its success. Strategic planning is important for an organization to focus on what is important for it to stay competitive.

→ HR departments develops their own subset goals and action plans that align with the overarching goals of the organization. The strategic HR plan addresses the same questions used during the larger strategic planning process. It should answer where the function is now, where it is heading (with the organization), how the team will get there, and how they will know that they are there.

→ As a result of the strategic planning process, an organization may decide that it needs to restructure itself in order to achieve its goals and remain competitive and viable in the marketplace. This includes mergers/acquisitions, divestitures, reductions in force, growth in force, or offshoring/outsourcing.

→ Managing ethics in the workplace holds tremendous benefit for stakeholders, and it greatly affects other key constituents including customers, employees, and the general public. Companies develop codes of ethics and values statements, have whistleblower policies and designate ethics officers to fulfill their commitment to ethical behavior.

→ Organizational design is the alignment of people, processes, compensation, and metrics with the strategy of the organization. Leaders and managers must make decisions about how to group people together to perform their work effectively.

→ Since the early 20th century, several categories leadership theories have developed: trait theories, behavioral theories, contingency theories, and power/influence theories

→ The objective of HR departments, essentially, is to recruit, retain, and motivate the best employees for the organization. To do so, they find ways to keep the company competitive in terms of its compensation, benefits, learning opportunities, career advancement, work/life balance, and other aspects that are important to employees.

→ HR generalists, also commonly called HR managers or HR business partners, have a broad range of responsibilities in one or more functional areas of human resources. Larger organizations typically have HR specialists with specific knowledge and skills.

→ To be influential in the organization, HR business partners need to position themselves as strategic advisors, champions for change, and operations managers. They must align themselves closely with the values of the organization and the visions of the leaders in order to be seen as valuable partners.

→ As organizations grow, they need to develop policies and procedures to maintain consistency throughout the organization, convey important information to employees, and stay compliant with federal and state laws. Documented policies can also protect the organization in the event of a lawsuit or complaint.

→ The Human Resource Information System (HRIS) is a type of HR management system or electronic platform for the data entry, tracking, and reporting needs of the human resources department. It should provide information on most data the company needs to track and analyze about applicants, employees, former employees.

→ HR metrics (measurements) can show important trends and information about the organization's people. This information can help leaders meet the needs of employees. There are a number of metrics that HR practitioners can track and analyze, such as turnover, time to hire, benefits utilization, and more.

→ HR helps the organization conduct its due diligence when evaluating a potential merger, plan a strategy for integrating the employees of the other company, and manage the change process.

Key Terms to Review

Acquisition

Behavioral theories of leadership

Bureaucratic leadership

Centralized decision making

Code of conduct

Code of ethics

Contingency theories of leadership

Core functions of an organization

Core Values

Corporate governance

Corporation

Decentralized decision making

Divestiture

Division of labor

Divisional structure

Expansion in force

External environment

Functional structure

Goals-based planning

Growth phases

HR business partner

HR generalist

HR Information System (HRIS)

HR metrics

HR policies

HR procedures

HR specialist

Human capital plan

Issues-based planning

Limited Liability Company

Matrix structure

Merger

Mission statement

Network structure

Offshoring

Organic planning

Organizational life cycle

Outsourcing

Partnership

PEST analysis

Porter's 5 Forces

Power and influence theories of leadership

Reduction in force

Restructuring

Sarbanes Oxley Act

Securities & Exchange Commission

Servant leadership

SMART goals

Sole proprietorship

Span of control

Statistical models

Strategic planning

Support functions of an organization

SWOT analysis

Team structure

Trait theories of leadership

Transformational leadership

Vision statement

Recruitment & Staffing Management

Section Overview

→ What is the doctrine of equal employment opportunity?

→ What laws prohibit discrimination in employment?

→ What is sexual harassment, and what should the organization do about it?

→ What reporting requirements do employers have with equal opportunity?

→ What is affirmative action, and how does it affect the employment practices of an organization?

→ What is the OFCCP's role in enforcing affirmative action laws?

→ How do HR practitioners analyze and document jobs?

→ What are the basic components of a job description?

→ How does HR plan for staffing needs throughout the year?

→ What steps are necessary to find new employees?

→ What is involved in onboarding employees?

→ What is succession planning, and how does it help organizations in the long term?

→ How do U.S. immigration laws impact employers?

Equal Employment Opportunity

The doctrine of Equal Employment Opportunity prohibits discrimination against applicants and employees because of certain personal characteristics, such as race, color, sex, and other protected classes. This doctrine attempts to ensure that all people have a fair opportunity in finding a job, being paid fairly, getting promoted, and having the same opportunities for development. Many federal, state, and local laws prohibit discrimination in employment. The following section describes the federal laws that mandate equal employment opportunities and are enforced by the federal Equal Employment Opportunity Commission[28].

Table: Federal Laws Prohibiting Discrimination in Employment

Federal Law	Protections
Title VII of the Civil Rights Act of 1964[29]	Prohibits discrimination on the basis of one's race, color, religion, national origin, or sex. Employers are required to reasonably accommodate applicants' and employees' sincerely held religious practices, unless doing so would impose an "undue hardship" on the business.
Pregnancy Discrimination Act[30]	Amends Title VII to prohibit discrimination against a woman because of pregnancy, childbirth, or a medical condition related to pregnancy or childbirth.
Equal Pay Act of 1963[31]	Makes it illegal to pay different wages to men and women if they perform equal work in the same workplace.
Age Discrimination in Employment Act of 1967[32]	Prohibits discrimination of applicants or employees based on age (over 40).

---

[28] Source: http://www.eeoc.gov/laws/statutes/

[29] Source: Title VII of the Civil Rights Act of 1964 (Title VII)

[30] Source: The Pregnancy Discrimination Act

[31] Source: The Equal Pay Act of 1963 (EPA)

[32] Source: The Age Discrimination in Employment Act of 1967 (ADEA)

Title I of the Americans with Disabilities Act of 1990[33]	Prohibits discrimination against a qualified person with a disability with respect to employment. Employers must reasonably accommodate the known physical or mental limitations of an otherwise qualified applicant or employee with a disability, unless doing so would impose an undue hardship on the business. (The Rehabilitation Act of 1973 prohibits discrimination of qualified employees or applicants with disabilities in the federal government.)
Genetic Information Nondiscrimination Act of 2008	Prohibits discrimination against employees or applicants because of genetic information. Genetic information includes information about an individual's genetic tests, the genetic tests of an individual's family members, or an individual's family medical history.

According to the laws listed above, federal law forbids discrimination in every aspect of employment, including hiring, compensation, discipline, and termination. It is also illegal to retaliate against a person because he or she reported discrimination, filed a charge of discrimination, or participated in an employment discrimination investigation or lawsuit. Employers are required to post notices describing the Federal laws prohibiting job discrimination based on race, color, religion, sex (including pregnancy), national origin, age (40 or older), disability or genetic information.

It is important to know that not all federal laws apply to all employers. Smaller employers (with less than a certain number of employees) may not be subject to nondiscrimination laws. Additionally, states and localities also have enacted their own nondiscrimination laws that certain employers must follow. Employers should monitor employment laws in all states in which they operate and determine how the laws apply to them.

Federal EEO laws also prohibit an employer from using employment policies and practices that have a disproportionately negative effect on applicants or employees of a protected class, if the policies or practices at issue are not job-related and necessary to the operation of the business. The laws also prohibit an employer from using employment policies and practices that have a disproportionately negative impact on applicants or employees age 40 or older, if the policies or practices are not based on a reasonable factor other than age. This concept of adverse effects on protected classes is called *disparate impact*.

---

[33] Source: Title I of the Americans with Disabilities Act of 1990 (ADA)

What Employers May Not Do

To comply with federal law, and to provide equal opportunity to all employees and applicants, employers may not do the following in their employment practices, based on one's race, color, religion, sex (including pregnancy), national origin, age (40 or older), disability or genetic information:

- Advertise a job that shows a preference based on a protected class.
- Recruit for new employees in a way that results in discrimination based on a protected class.
- Discriminate against an applicant or refuse to give an application to a certain protected class.
- Require pre-employment or post-employment examinations that may be inherently discriminatory.
- Take into account a person's characteristic (protected class) when making decisions about job referrals.
- Make decisions about job assignments or promotions based on an employee's protected class.
- Discriminate in the way employees are paid, based on protected class.
- Consider an employee's protected class when taking a disciplinary action.
- Refuse a reasonable accommodation to a disabled employee, unless doing so would cause an undue hardship to business operations.
- Refuse to accommodate one's sincerely held religious beliefs, and attendance at religious services, unless doing so would cause a substantial burden to the business.

Harassment

The same laws that prohibit discrimination also prohibit harassment based on one's protected class. Harassment can take the form of slurs, graffiti, offensive or derogatory comments, or other verbal or physical conduct. It is also illegal to harass someone because they have complained about discrimination, filed a charge of discrimination, or participated in an employment discrimination investigation or lawsuit.

Sexual harassment is a specific type of harassment that includes unwelcome sexual advances, requests for sexual favors, and other conduct of a sexual nature. Although the law does not forbid simple teasing, occasional comments, or isolated incidents that are not serious, harassment is illegal if it is so pervasive or severe that it creates a hostile or offensive work environment, or if it results in an adverse employment decision, such as termination or demotion of a victim.

Sexual harassment can take many forms in a workplace, and any conduct of a sexual nature that makes an employee uncomfortable has the potential to be sexual harassment. The harasser can be the victim's supervisor, a supervisor in another area, a co-worker, or someone who is not an employee of the employer, such as a client or customer. Harassment outside of the workplace may also be illegal if there is a link with the workplace. For example, if a supervisor harasses an employee while driving the employee to a meeting. For these reasons, organizations typically develop strict policies against harassment with detailed procedures to report, investigate, and handle complaints[34].

Dress Code

In general, an employer may lawfully establish a dress code that applies to all employees or employees within certain job categories, with a few possible exceptions.

While a dress code may conflict with some workers' beliefs or practices, it must not punish employees because of their national origin. For example, an employer may not prohibit certain ethnic attire while allowing casual attire. In addition, if the dress code conflicts with an employee's religious practices and the employee requests an accommodation, the employer must make an exception or modification to the dress code unless doing so would result in undue hardship. (The same rule applies to employees with disabilities who request a reasonable accommodation.)

Constructive Discharge/Forced To Resign

Under federal law, it may also be considered a discriminatory practice when an employer forces an employee to resign or makes the work environment so intolerable that a reasonable person could not sustain employment. This is called constructive discharge.

---

[34] Source: http://www.eeoc.gov/laws/practices/inquiries_medical.cfm

The Equal Employment Opportunity Commission

The U.S. Equal Employment Opportunity Commission enforces federal laws prohibiting employment discrimination. An employee or job applicant (complainant) who believes that he or she has been discriminated against at work can file a "Charge of Discrimination."

Not all employers are covered by the laws the EEOC enforces, and not all employees are protected. This can vary depending on the type of employer, the number of employees it has, and the type of discrimination alleged. Filing an EEO complaint does not automatically mean the company has committed any wrongdoing; instead, it is a formal allegation that an employer has discriminated against the complainant. It is the role of the EEOC's to investigate the matter to determine whether there is reasonable cause to believe that discrimination has occurred.

All of the laws enforced by EEOC, except for the Equal Pay Act, require complainants to file a Charge of Discrimination with the agency before they can file a job discrimination lawsuit against their employer. In addition, there are strict time limits for filing a charge.

EEO Reporting Requirements

Federal law requires employers to keep certain employment records. The EEOC also collects workforce data from some employers (with more than 100 employees in the private sector), regardless of whether a charge has been filed against the company. The data is typically collected using a standardized EEO-1 report and is used for a variety of purposes including enforcement of laws, self-assessment of equal employment opportunity by employers, and other federal research. Although company's specific data remains confidential, aggregated data is available to the public.

Affirmative action is the policy of providing opportunities specifically for, and favoring members of, a disadvantaged minority group who have historically suffered discrimination. In the United States, under Executive Order 11248; Section 503 of the Rehabilitation Act of 1973; and Section 4212 of the Vietnam Era Veteran's Readjustment Assistance Act, government contractors and subcontractors must provide affirmative actions when recruiting, hiring, and employing qualified minorities, women, people with disabilities, and covered veterans. Altogether, these policies ban discrimination and require Federal contractors and subcontractors to take affirmative action to ensure that all individuals have an equal opportunity for employment, without regard to race, color, religion, sex, national origin, disability or status as a Vietnam era or special disabled veteran.

"Affirmative actions" may include specific outreach to minority candidates, special training programs, and other positive steps to ensure a diverse workforce. Employers who are subject to affirmative action typically develop formalized affirmative action plans and policies. These plans are reviewed annually and documentation is maintained to ensure compliance with federal rules and regulations[35].

The OFCCP

The U.S. Department of Labor's Office of Federal Contract Compliance Programs (OFCCP) enforces the affirmative action laws, regulations, and executive orders. As a condition of maintaining a contract with the federal government, the OFCCP requires a contractor to provide for affirmative action and non-discrimination and employment. The OFCCEP routinely investigates contractors' employment practices and investigate complaints of discrimination. Failure to comply with the non-discrimination or affirmative action provisions of federal law is a violation of the contract. A contractor found to be in violation may have its contracts terminated or suspended, and the contractor may be deemed ineligible for future government contracts.

---

[35] Source: http://www.dol.gov/dol/topic/hiring/affirmativeact.htm

Affirmative Action Requirements

Under Executive Order 11246, non-construction contractors with 50 or more employees and government contracts of $50,000 or more are required to develop and implement a written affirmative action plan (AAP). An AAP is defined as a set of employment procedures to which a contractor commits itself to apply every good faith effort. The plan is kept on file and carried out by the contractor, and it is submitted to OFCCP only if the agency requests it for an audit.

The AAP identifies those areas, if any, in the contractor's workforce that reflect utilization of women and minorities. Under-utilization occurs when fewer minorities or women occupy a particular job group than would reasonably be expected based on their availability. Availability is determined by the predominance of women and minorities in the geographical location of the company or site, who have the bona fide qualifications for the job. Based on utilization analyses of the availability of qualified individuals, contractors must establish goals to reduce or overcome under-utilization. Employers are expected to consider the candidacy of women and minorities, when they are qualified, and provide employment opportunities and advancement. However, employment decisions are to be made on a non-discriminatory basis.

For contractors in the construction industry, the OFCCP has established a distinct approach to affirmative action due to the seasonal and temporary nature of the construction workforce. For these businesses, the OFCCP, rather than the contractor, assigns goals and affirmative actions that must be undertaken. For example, a goal of 6.9 percent of females employed by the company was developed in 1980 and continues to be effective today. The regulations also specify the good faith steps construction contractors must take in order to increase the hiring of minorities and women.

Developing Affirmative Action Plans

An Affirmative Action plan or program (AAP) is a tool employers develop and use to achieve their affirmative action goals. AAPs contain methods to measure and evaluate the composition of the workforce (i.e., demographic makeup) of the organization and compare it to the relative composition of the available labor pools (e.g., in the same geographic region). An AAP also ensures equal employment opportunity by embedding this philosophy into the organization's employment practices, employment decisions, compensation programs, and performance management systems. Affirmative Action plans also include practical steps an organization will take when people of certain demographics are underutilized. Employers typically audit and report on their affirmative action plans on an annual basis, measuring their progress toward achieving the goals of affirmative action.

Goals of Affirmative Action Plans

Affirmative Action plans typically outline a goal-setting process that is used to target and measure the effectiveness of affirmative action efforts to prevent and eliminate discrimination. However, according to federal regulations, the OFCCP may not penalize contractors for not meeting goals. It is prohibited for employers to establish racial quotas and engage in preferential treatment of certain groups (including women and minorities).

Job Analysis & Job Descriptions

A major component of effective human resource management is job analysis and job documentation. Every position within an organization should have a corresponding job description that accurately and completely describes the job. At its very basic, the job description is a document that provides an overview of the position's major responsibilities, and identifies the knowledge, skills and abilities that are necessary to perform the job. The document may also communicate the expected results of the position and explain how performance is evaluated. A job description, however, does not need to include every detail of how the work is performed. The following table lists the major components of a job description:

Section	Purpose	Examples
General Information	Basic position and pay information, which may also be tracked in the HR Information System (HRIS)	Job title Position Type (e.g., Full Time) FLSA Status Pay Grade Department Direct Supervisor Direct Reports Job Code
Position Purpose	A summary of the position's essential functions and its role in relation to the department or organizational unit	Description of the role Relation to the department or organization Estimated duration of position
Essential Job Duties	A list of duties and responsibilities. An essential function occupies a significant amount of the position's time and requires specialized skills to perform.	Functions of the job, arranged by importance and percentage of time spent Essential tasks inter-related to the accomplishment of an essential function.
Minimum Requirements	The knowledge, skills, and abilities required to perform the essential functions of the job.	Education Length of experience Soft skills Technical skills Specific experience

Job Analysis

The process of understanding a job and developing a job description is called job analysis. There are many ways that HR practitioners can perform a job analysis, but typically, this process involves interviews with the incumbent of a position, his/her manager, and those who work closely with the position. HR professionals can use a combination of interviews, job shadowing, questionnaires, and sample job descriptions to develop job descriptions for the organization. However, it is important that the job description accurately reflect the essential duties and bona fide requirements of the job.

Staffing Plans and the Recruitment Process

Staff planning is a process by which an organization ensures it employs the right number of qualified people with particular skills to achieve organizational goals and objectives. Staffing plans involve the cooperation of senior leadership, human resources, and management. The following list describes the various components of a staff planning program[36]:

- Job descriptions

- Skills assessment of the current workforce (identifying gaps)

- Turnover trends to predict how many people will leave an organization

- Business trends examining both internal changes and the external factors.

Once all relevant information has been collected, the human resources department (or staffing department in larger organizations) can forecast its staffing and recruitment needs. Typically, HR or staffing professionals work directly with business unit leads to interpret staffing metrics and forecast staffing data for the fiscal year.

During the planning process, HR and business unit leads will discuss the needs of the business unit, re-evaluate jobs and processes, and identify a staffing model that supports the goals of the business unit. In some cases, a job may be redesigned, combined with another job, or divided into two or more jobs. The needs of the business as well as the available budget will determine how jobs are structured and how many staff a particular business unit can have during the year.

Recruitment Process

Once the organization has developed a staffing plan, it will implement it throughout the year. As jobs become available (through turnover or growth), organizations will recruit candidates for these vacancies. The following is an overview of a typical recruitment process. Depending on the size, complexity, and culture of the organization, these steps may be more detailed or abbreviated.

---

[36] Source: http://www.shrm.org/TemplatesTools/hrqa/Pages/Howdowedevelopastaffingplan.aspx

Steps of the Recruitment Process

1. Decide upon the recruitment process for the position: how many candidates will be identified, estimated timeline for filling the position, number of interviews, and composition of interviewing team.

2. Create or revise job descriptions to accurately reflect the essential functions and requirements of the job.

3. Develop a job ad based on the job description that includes information about the company, salary range, preferred requirements, and/or benefits.

4. Identify candidate sources and begin the search. Post job ads to job boards, social media, newspapers/classifieds, universities/colleges, and other places where qualified candidates may be reached. Internal postings on a company intranet or bulletin board (for referrals) may be another method used. Advertisements should include instructions for applying (e.g., an email address to submit resumes, or an online application system).

5. Pre-screen resumes and identify applicants who meet the qualifications of the job. Develop a short list of candidates for further consideration.

6. Conduct an initial phone screen of shortlisted candidates, ask questions to understand qualifications, gauge interest, and evaluate the candidates' potential. Trim down shortlist of candidates to a few to bring in for an interview.

7. Interview candidates (with interviewing team) and ask probing questions to further evaluate qualifications and fit for the position. In some cases, a second or even third interview is conducted for the finalist(s).

8. Conduct pre-employment tests and background checks of finalist(s) if necessary for the position or a requirement of the organization.

9. Make an offer of employment to the final candidate, which includes details of salary, job role, responsibilities, benefits, start date, and other relevant information. In some cases, a verbal offer is made over the telephone and followed up by a written letter. Regardless, it is a best practice to always send a written offer with the terms of employment and have it signed by the candidate.

10. In some cases, the candidate may negotiate salary, benefits, perks, office location, and other factors. When an agreement has been made, it is also a best practice to update the written offer letter and have the candidate sign it.

Once the candidate has accepted the terms, and is preparing to begin working for the organization, the organization should take steps to ensure that the new employee is transitioned and integrated into the organization properly.

Onboarding

Once new employees are hired, they typically go through onboarding or new hire training. Onboarding is the process of helping new hires integrate into their new work environment, learn their jobs, and transition into their roles. Done effectively, onboarding is a critical component of the overall recruitment process for the employer and the employee. Onboarding activities typically involve the following:

- Tour of office or facility

- Organizational overview – explaining the history, products/services, and strategy/vision

- Completion of required HR and payroll forms, as well as benefits enrollment (if applicable)

- Training on the rules, culture, and procedures of the organization

- On the job training and job shadowing

- Mandated training on safety, sexual harassment, nondiscrimination, whistleblower, and other topics as required by law.

While onboarding is typically only offered in many organizations for only a day up to a couple weeks, a robust onboarding process spans one to two years. This lengthier onboarding process will monitor the employee's progress, provide mechanisms for ongoing feedback, and help the employee understand how they fit into the greater "picture" of the organization. For many organizations, this lengthy onboarding process is simply integrated into their overall performance management program.

Depending on the structure, size, and resources of the organization, onboarding programs can be simple or complex but should address at minimum the logistics, training, and safety of the new employee. New employees should have ample time training on their job, and shadowing others if possible, to gain an understanding of the overall flow of the product or service. Having this holistic understanding of the organization and its operations, as well as a foundation of knowledge of their jobs, new employees are better positioned to be successful in the long term.

Succession Planning

In order to remain viable and competitive, organizations need to ensure that they retain key talent to lead, manage, and carry out the organization's mission and vision. As employees resign, retire, or otherwise turnover, it is important for the organization to plan so that key positions are constantly filled with the most qualified people.

Succession planning is an organization's systematic approach to:

- Build a pool of future leaders to ensure leadership continuity

- Develop potential successors of leadership

- Identify the best candidates for certain types of positions (for future needs)

- Allocate resources to develop internal talent and create meaningful career paths.

Succession planning recognizes that some jobs are critical to the organization and therefore must be filled by the most qualified persons. Effectively done, succession planning is critical to mission success and creates an effective process for recognizing, developing, and retaining top leadership talent.

The Succession Planning Process[37]

1. *Align strategic planning with workforce planning.* Identify the long-term vision and direction of the organization, and analyze future needs to develop and offer products and services. Use data to understand the current composition of the workforce and make projections for future workforce needs.

2. *Analyze gaps in future workforce needs.* Identify needs for competencies or skills, and determine talent needed for future demands. Develop a business plan that is based on long-term talent needs rather than specific positions.

3. *Identify talent pools of current workforce and categorize talent based on their career levels, paths, and potential.* Assess the competencies and skills of employees using

---

[37] Source: https://www.opm.gov/policy-data-oversight/human-capital-management/reference-materials/leadership-knowledge-management/successionplanning.pdf

formal appraisals and 360-degree feedback. Analyze external sources of future leadership as well.

4. *Develop strategies for succession,* including recruitment, relocation, and retention programs. Identify learning and development strategies, including job assignments, training programs, job shadowing, coaching and mentoring, and feedback mechanisms.

5. *Implement succession-planning strategies.* Maintain commitment and involvement of senior leadership. Communicate activities with employees regularly and actively.

6. *Monitor and evaluate succession-planning efforts.* Solicit and consider feedback from leadership as well as potential future leaders. Analyze employee satisfaction through surveys and informal feedback. Assess the responsiveness of the organization to change and future needs.

Benefits of Succession Planning

There are several factors typically found in successful succession planning initiatives. For example:

- It is based on the long-term needs of the business and is an investment in the future.
- Senior leadership is invested in the process and help to groom emerging leaders.
- Future leaders are accountable for their own self-development.
- The pipeline of future leadership is based on anticipated needs.
- Success is based on a business case for long-term needs.
- Careful analysis of the organization's workforce and needs guide the process.
- The process creates meaningful career paths for employees, which can be a motivational tool.
- It addresses workforce challenges such as recruitment and retention.

Immigration Issues

Under the Immigration Reform and Control Act of 1986 (IRCA), it is illegal for an employer to hire any person who is not legally authorized to work in the United States. Employers are required to verify the employment eligibility of all new employees. For organizations of certain sizes, the IRCA also prohibits discrimination based on national origin (as does Title VII) as well as on citizenship status. The law seeks to prevent employers from discriminating against job applicants who may look or sound foreign. The United States Citizenship and Immigration Services (USCIS), a component of the United States Department of Homeland Security, oversees and enforces immigration including that which is employment related.

Hiring an alien for employment if you know that the alien is unauthorized is unlawful. The law defines an "unauthorized alien" as one who is not lawfully admitted for permanent residence in the U.S., or who is not authorized to be employed in the U.S.[38] One way employers avoid noncompliance with the law is to hire U.S. citizens. A U.S. citizen is not an alien (and therefore not an unauthorized alien). Another way of avoiding noncompliance is to hire authorized aliens, such as permanent residents – individuals who have a "green card" – or those aliens who are authorized to work in certain conditions (through a work visa). Below is a chart of the various types of work visas available to immigrant workers.

TABLE: Types of Temporary Work Visas (Sample)

Visa category	General description
H-1B	**Person in Specialty Occupation.** Requires a college degree or its equivalent.
H-2A	**Temporary Agricultural Worker.** For temporary or seasonal agricultural work. Limited to immigrants from designated countries.
H-2B	**Temporary Non-agricultural Worker.** For temporary or seasonal non-agricultural work. Limited to immigrants from designated countries.
L	**Intracompany Transferee.** To work at a particular entity or location of the current employer in a managerial or executive role, or in a position requiring specialized knowledge. Requires 1 year of continuous employment by current employer within the past 3 years.

---

[38] Source: http://www.techrepublic.com/blog/10-things/10-tips-for-complying-with-immigration-law-when-hiring-staff/

O	**Individual with Extraordinary Ability or Achievement.** For immigrant workers with extraordinary ability or achievement in business, science, arts, athletics, education, and other categories. Must demonstrate national or international acclaim and continue to work in their field of expertise. This category also includes people providing essential services in support of a worker in this category.

In general, a citizen of a foreign country who wishes to enter the United States must first obtain a visa (for a temporary stay or permanent residence). Temporary worker visas are specifically for people who want to enter the United States to work for a specific period of time (rather than permanently or indefinitely). Applications for all visas require the prospective employer to file a petition with U.S. Citizenship and Immigration Services (USCIS). The petition must be approved in order for the visa to be issued. Hiring immigrants with approved visas is compliant with federal law, while hiring immigrants without authorization from USCIS is illegal and can result in substantial penalties.

USCIS Form I-9

Form I-9 is a government-issued form that documents the evidence the new employee provides to show authorization to work in the United States. It also certifies the employer's actions taken to verify the evidence. This form must be completed within the first three days of the employee's hire. However, if the employment is for less than three days, the form must be completed on the day of hire.

To validate an employee's ability to work, an employer's authorized representative must verify both the identity of the employee and the employee's legal ability to work. Depending on the specific documents provided, one or two may be required. Some documents, such as a U.S. passport, prove both identity and authorization to work (categorized under "List A" of acceptable documents). Other documents, such as a driver's license, prove identity but do not prove authorization to work (List B of acceptable documents). Others such as certain Social Security cards, prove authorization to work but do not prove identity (List C). The instructions on the form indicate which documents are acceptable and which combination(s) of documents may be used to verify employment eligibility. Documentation regarding I-9 verification must be kept for certain minimum periods of time as mandated by law -- either for three years from the employee's date of hire or one year after the employee leaves -- whichever occurs later.

E-Verify

E-Verify is an internet-based system (run by the federal government) that allows employers to verify a person's employment eligibility electronically. It is intended to serve as a supplement to completion of Form I-9. Participation in E-Verify is voluntary for employers, unless the company is a certain type of federal contractor or otherwise is required to by law. Employers may only use E-Verify after making a hiring decision; it is not lawful to use it for screening applicants or using for other purposes not connected to verifying employment eligibility.

The E-Verify system will confirm the individual's eligibility to work in the United States. If the system reports a "tentative non-confirmation" (TNC) for a new hire, it means that that the system found possible problems in verifying the person's eligibility to work in the US. In that situation, the employee may contest the TNC, and the employer may not take adverse actions against that person during the period of challenging the TNC. If it is determined, however, that the employee is in fact not eligible to work in the US, the employer may no longer continue to employ the individual.

Main Ideas to Remember

→ The doctrine of Equal Employment Opportunity prohibits discrimination against applicants and employees because of certain personal characteristics, such as race, color, sex, and other protected classes. This doctrine attempts to ensure that all people have a fair opportunity in finding a job, being paid fairly, getting promoted, and having the same opportunities for development.

→ Federal laws that prohibit employment discrimination include Title VII of the Civil Rights Act of 1964; Pregnancy Discrimination Act; Equal Pay Act of 1963; Age Discrimination in Employment Act of 1967; and Title I of the Americans with Disabilities Act of 1990. Many states have their own nondiscrimination laws, too.

→ Harassment can take the form of slurs, graffiti, offensive or derogatory comments, or other verbal or physical conduct. It is also illegal to harass someone because they have complained about discrimination, filed a charge of discrimination, or participated in an employment discrimination investigation or lawsuit.

→ Sexual harassment is a specific type of harassment that includes unwelcome sexual advances, requests for sexual favors, and other conduct of a sexual nature. Harassment is illegal if it is so pervasive or severe that it creates a hostile or offensive work environment, or if it results in an adverse employment decision, such as termination or demotion of a victim. Organizations typically develop strict policies against harassment with detailed procedures to report, investigate, and handle complaints.

→ The Equal Opportunity Commission enforces federal laws prohibiting employment discrimination. It also collects workforce data from some employers (EEO-1 report) for a variety of purposes including enforcement of laws, self-assessment of equal employment opportunity by employers, and other federal research.

→ Affirmative action is the policy of providing opportunities specifically for, and favoring members of, a disadvantaged minority group who have historically suffered discrimination. "Affirmative actions" may include specific outreach to minority candidates, special training programs, and other positive steps to ensure a diverse workforce. Employers who are subject to affirmative action typically develop formalized affirmative action plans and policies.

→ The U.S. Department of Labor's Office of Federal Contract Compliance Programs (OFCCP) enforces the affirmative action laws, regulations, and executive orders. As a condition of maintaining a contract with the federal government, the OFCCP requires a contractor to provide for affirmative action and non-discrimination and employment.

→ An Affirmative Action plan or program (AAP) is a tool employers develop and use to achieve their affirmative action goals. AAP's contain methods to measure and evaluate the composition of the workforce (i.e., demographic makeup) of the organization and compare it to the relative composition of the available labor pools (e.g., in the same geographic region). An AAP also ensures equal employment opportunity by embedding this philosophy into the organization's employment practices, employment decisions, compensation programs, and performance management systems.

→ The process of understanding a job and developing a job description is called job analysis. HR professionals can use a combination of interviews, job shadowing, questionnaires, and sample job descriptions to develop job descriptions for the organization.

→ A job description is a document that provides an overview of the position's major responsibilities, and identifies the knowledge, skills and abilities that are necessary to perform the job. The document may also communicate the expected results of the position and explain how performance is evaluated.

→ Staff planning is a process by which an organization ensures it employs the right number of qualified people with particular skills to achieve organizational goals and objectives. Staffing plans involve the cooperation of senior leadership, human resources, and management. During the planning process, HR and business unit leads will discuss the needs of the business unit, re-evaluate jobs and processes, and identify a staffing model that supports the goals of the business unit.

→ As jobs become available, organizations will recruit candidates for these vacancies. The recruitment process includes steps such as posting the job, collecting and screening resumes, pre-interviewing candidates, interviewing candidates, administering pre-employment tests and background checks, and presenting offers of employment.

→ Onboarding is the process of helping new hires integrate into their new work environment, learn their jobs, and transition into their roles. Done effectively, onboarding is a critical component of the overall recruitment process for the employer and the employee.

→ Succession planning is a process by which an organization plans and grooms future leadership, so that key positions are constantly filled with the most qualified people.

→ Under the Immigration Reform and Control Act of 1986 (IRCA), it is illegal for an employer to hire any person who is not legally authorized to work in the United States.

Employers are required to verify the employment eligibility of all new employees. Form I-9 is a government issued form that documents the evidence the new employee provides to show authorization to work in the United States.

→ E-Verify is an internet-based system (run by the federal government) that allows employers to verify a person's employment eligibility electronically. It is intended to serve as a supplement to completion of Form I-9.

Key Terms to Review

Affirmative Action	Job analysis
Affirmative action plan	Job description
Age Discrimination in Employment Act of 1967	OFCCP
Background check	Onboarding
Constructive discharge	Phone screen
EEO-1 Report	Pre-employment testing
EEOC	Pregnancy Discrimination Act
Equal Employment Opportunity	Reasonable accommodation
Equal Pay Act of 1963	Recruitment process
E-Verify	Retaliation
Executive Order 11246	Sexual Harassment
Genetic Information Nondiscrimination Act of 2008	Staffing plan
	Succession planning
Harassment	Title I of the American with Disabilities Act
I-9 Form	Title VII of the Civil Rights Act of 1964
Immigration Reform and Control Act	Work visas (and types)

Total Rewards

What are Total Rewards?

"Total Rewards" describe all the tools an employer uses to attract, motivate, and retain employees. This includes anything the employee perceives to be valuable as a result of working at the organization[39]. There are five components of total rewards:

---

[39] Source: https://www.worldatwork.org/aboutus/html/aboutus-whatis.jsp

Depending on available resources, employers offer these various programs or components as part of a total compensation package to employees. Delivering an appropriate and competitive total compensation package is key to retaining and motivating employees, who in turn will deliver performance and results for the organization. In order to remain competitive, the organization should continually monitor the packages of its competitors and overall industry. Salary and benefit surveys are reliable sources of data to which the organization can benchmark its compensation and benefit programs.

Compensation

Employee compensation refers to the cash compensation that an employee receives in exchange for the work they perform. Typically, cash compensation consists of a wage or salary, and includes any commissions or bonuses. Cash compensation can be categorized as fixed pay, variable pay, or premium pay.

Types of Compensation

- *Fixed pay (or base pay)* - nondiscretionary compensation that does not fluctuate based on performance or results. It is linked to the organization's pay philosophy and structure, as well as market conditions. <u>Examples: Salary pay, hourly wage</u>

- Variable pay – compensation that changes directly with performance or results achieved. It is a payment based on a performance over a specified period of time, and can be linked to either or both the employee's and employer's performance. <u>Examples: Commissions, bonuses, short-term incentives, stock options, performance-sharing incentives, profit sharing</u>

- *Premium pay* – compensation that is tied to nontraditional work schedules, shifts, and skills; provided in addition to fixed pay. <u>Examples: Shift differential pay, weekend/holiday pay, on-call pay, skills-based pay</u>

Pay Structures

A company's pay structure is the method of administering its pay philosophy. The two most common types of pay structures are the **internal equity method**, which pays based on the job's placement in the organizational hierarchy, and **market pricing**, in which each job's pay is tied to the prevailing market rate.

A pay structure helps clarify the relative value the organization places on each role, and why employees are compensated differently. It also helps human resources personnel to equitably administer the organization's overall pay philosophy. For example, an organization may want to pay everyone at market; or it may decide to pay some people at market and some above it. Additionally, the pay structure also helps HR professionals administer incentive compensation, especially for people with higher levels of responsibility and accountability[40].

---

[40] Source: http://www.salary.com/pay-structures/

To establish pay structures and determine the appropriate pay levels for jobs, HR professionals typically conduct a compensation analysis as pictured on the next page:

Start with payroll budget.

Research merit increases and salary adjustments in company and overall industry.	Determine how many jobs need to be priced.	Project upcoming payroll budgets to account for these adjustments.

Benchmark each job's value.

Use salary surveys to match compensation of internal job to external job with similar duties. It is best to compare to other jobs in the same industry or geographical location.	Determine the benchmarked value based on the organization's compesnation philosophy. For example, if the organization decides to pay "at market," the 50th percentile should be looked at.

Create salary ranges and pay grades.

Use internal equity method to create a series of grades or bands, with wide ranges at the top of the structure and narrower ranges at the bottom. Each grade is tied to a different level of responsibility within the company.	Pay grades should have a s pread by which the employee can progress in his/her job. There should be a minimum and maximum for each pay grade. Typically, the midpoint of a given grade should be 15% higher than that of the lower grade.	Slot jobs into pay grades based on their market value and/or relative value in the organization.

Executive Compensation

To attract and retain the most qualified executive team, organizations sometimes offer a unique package of executive benefits and compensation for presidents, C-level executives, vice presidents, and senior directors. Executive compensation differs from packages offered to lower-level employees. Executive compensation packages often include:

- Base salary
- Bonuses or performance incentives
- Signing bonus for joining the organization
- Stock options
- Income protection in the event of a company sale or liquidation
- Predetermined severance package for termination without cause
- Additional executive-only benefits such additional insurance coverage
- Company perquisites (perks)

As with any other compensation, executive compensation is negotiated between the potential executive and the employer. However, the structure or terms may be substantially different from the "regular" package offered to other employees, and it may be specifically customized for the executive (e.g., different structure from that offered to other executives). Typically, executive salary and benefits are documented in the form of an employment contract or agreement. This document outlines the terms of employment including the full spectrum of compensation, benefits, perks, performance incentives, and severance agreements. In contrast with an offer letter provided to a lower-level employee offer letter, executive compensation agreements are more detailed and contain a variety of benefits and perks not offered to other levels of employees.

Benefits

Employee benefits are important to the livelihood of employees and their families. The benefits that an organization offers to employees not only help the employees with their health, financial, and personal needs, but it can also make a total compensation package competitive and rich. The benefits an employer offers can also be a deciding factor for a talented individual's decision to work at the organization.

There are two categories of employee benefits: those that must be provided by law (also called mandated benefits) and those which the employer chooses to offer as a way to compensate employees (or comply with a collective bargaining agreement in a unionized environment). Examples of required benefits include worker's compensation and unemployment insurance, while optional benefits include health insurance coverage and retirement plans.

Mandated Benefits

The following table provides an overview benefits that are mandated by law. Note that some states may require additional benefits for workers in those states[41].

Mandated Benefit	What It's For
Social Security Taxes	Requires employers to pay Social Security taxes at the same rate paid by their employees, which is used to fund retirement income.
Unemployment Insurance	Provides unemployment benefits to eligible workers who are unemployed through no fault of their own and meet other eligibility requirements as determined by state law. Each State administers a separate unemployment insurance program within guidelines established by Federal law.
Workers' Compensation Insurance	Workers Compensation benefits are provided when an employee becomes injured or ill in connection with his or her job. Benefits include payment for lost wages and payment of medical bills. Requires employers to carry Workers' Compensation Insurance coverage through an insurance carrier, on a self-insured basis, or through the state's program.
Disability Insurance	Certain states require businesses to provide insurance for wage loss due to employees' non-work related sickness or injury. These benefits provide partial income replacement during the period of disability.

---

[41]Source: http://www.sba.gov/content/required-employee-benefits

Family and Medical Leave	The Family and Medical Leave Act (FMLA) provides up to 12 weeks of job-protected, unpaid leave during any 12-month period to eligible, covered employees for the following reasons:
	1) birth and care of the eligible employee's child, or placement for adoption or foster care of a child with the employee;
	2) care of an immediate family member (spouse, child, parent) who has a serious health condition; or
	3) care of the employee's own serious health condition.
	The law also requires that employee's group health benefits be maintained during the leave.
Military Family Leave (FMLA)	The FMLA was amended in 2008 to provide protections specifically for military families. For eligible, covered employees, up to 26 weeks of military caregiver leave (to care for injured family members), and up to 12 weeks of qualifying exigency leave (to tend to matters related to deployment). These leaves are also unpaid; however, the employee's group health benefits must be maintained during the leave.
Patient Protection and Affordable Care Act (PPACA)	PPACA requires certain employers to provide affordable health insurance that provides minimum value to their full-time employees (and their dependents),

Health & Welfare Benefits

Health and welfare benefits are the most common discretionary benefits offered by employers. These benefits are typically offered in the form of a group health plan established or maintained by the employer (or union), and provides medical care for participants (and often their dependents) directly or through insurance, reimbursement, or otherwise. The following are health and welfare benefits that employers may offer to their employees as part of their total compensation package:

- Medical Plan
- Dental Plan
- Vision Plan
- Prescription Drug Plan – provides
- Flexible Spending Account (FSA)
- Health Reimbursement Account (HRA)

- Health Savings Account (HSA)

- Life Insurance

- Accidental Death & Dismemberment Insurance

- Short- and Long-Term Disability Insurance

Most welfare plans can be provided by an employer to its employees on a pre-tax basis (meaning the cost of the plan is not taxable to the employee). As an exception to this general rule, some welfare plans will result in additional gross income to a highly compensated employee or a key employee unless the plan meets the nondiscrimination requirements determined by the Internal Revenue Code.

Words to Know

Cafeteria Plan

A cafeteria plan (also called a Code section 125 plan or a flexible benefits plan) allows an employee to reduce his or her compensation in order to pay his or her share for employer-provided benefits coverage on a pre-tax basis. To qualify, a cafeteria plan must allow employees to choose from a selection of two or more benefits consisting of cash or qualified benefit plans. Under a cafeteria plan, an employee may obtain pre-tax benefits as health insurance, group-term life insurance, flexible spending accounts, and certain voluntary supplemental benefits (e.g., dental) through the plan. A cafeteria plan must not discriminate in favor of either highly compensated employees or key employees.

Flexible Spending Account (FSA)

A flexible spending account allows an employee to set aside a portion of earnings to pay for qualified expenses as established in the cafeteria plan. An FSA is most commonly for medical expenses but is also used for dependent care or other expenses. FSA contributions are made on a pre-tax basis.

Health Reimbursement Account (HRA)

A health reimbursement account is an employer-funded account that can be used to pay for qualified medical expenses of the employee and his/her dependents. This account may be used to pay for the participant's out-of-pocket, qualified medical expenses until insurance covers the expense or the funds are depleted.

Health Savings Account (HSA)

A health savings account is a pre-tax medical savings account available to participants in a high-deductible health plan (HDHP). The funds contributed to an account are not subject to federal income tax upon deposit. Funds are used to pay for the participant's out-of-pocket, qualified medical expenses (and those of his/her legal dependents).

There are a number of federal laws by which employers (as plan administrators and/or fiduciaries) and health plans must comply. Below are some of the most predominant federal laws that apply to health and welfare benefits:

- *Employee Retirement Income Security Act (ERISA)* – covers most private sector health plans. ERISA provides protections for participants and beneficiaries covered under employee benefit plans. Plan administrators and fiduciaries are required to meet certain standards of conduct that are outlined in the law.

- *Consolidated Omnibus Budget Reconciliation Act (COBRA)* - grants employees the right to pay premiums for and keep the group health insurance that they would otherwise lose after they quit or lose their jobs, or reduce their work hours. Most people can retain their insurance coverage for up to 18 months (and longer in some situations).

- *Health Insurance Portability and Accountability Act of 1996 (HIPAA)* – provides opportunities for people to retain (or obtain) health insurance during qualifying events; protects the confidentiality and security of healthcare information; and provides mechanisms to control administrative costs[42].

- *Patient Protection and Affordable Care Act* – in general, requires certain employers to provide affordable health insurance that provides minimum value to their full-time employees (and their dependents), to communicate about health-care marketplaces to employees, and to provide a standardized summary of coverage to employees (among other requirements); requires insurers to cover pre-existing conditions and cover all applicants[43]. (Note: Many other components to the PPACA are not listed here. Check with the U.S. Department of Health and Human Services for complete information.)

---

[42] Source: http://en.wikipedia.org/wiki/Health_Insurance_Portability_and_Accountability_Act

[43] Source: http://www.hhs.gov/healthcare/rights/

- *Pregnancy Discrimination Act* – requires certain health plans to provide the same level of coverage for pregnancy as for other conditions.

- *Mental Health Parity Act* – requires that when a health plan covers mental health services, the annual or lifetime dollar limits, copays, and treatment limitations must be the same or higher than the limits for other medical benefits[44].

- *Americans with Disabilities Act* – among other protections, requires that disabled and non-disabled individuals must be provided the same benefits, premiums, deductibles, and limits under a given health plan.

- *Family and Medical Leave Act* – among other protections, requires that an employer maintain health coverage for a qualified employee for the duration of FMLA leave.

- *Uniformed Services Employment and Reemployment Rights Act (USERRA)* – among other protections, allows employees to continue group health coverage while absent from work due to military service.

Retirement Benefits

In addition to health and welfare plans, many organizations also offer retirement plans to their employees. A **retirement plan** is a savings arrangement designed to replace employment income upon retirement. These plans may be set up by employers, unions, or other institutions. Retirement plans fall under three types of categories: defined benefit plan, defined contribution plan, and profit sharing plan.

- *Defined Benefit Plan* - a company-provided pension plan in which an employee's pension payments are calculated (defined) according to their length of service with the company and their earnings prior to retirement.

- *Defined Contribution Plan* - a retirement savings plan in which the employer, employee (or both) contributes on a regular basis (typically pre-tax assuming certain conditions are met). There is no guaranteed benefit. The employee accesses his or her account upon retirement.

- *Profit Sharing Plan* – typically offered in conjunction with a defined contribution plan, it allows the company to allocate profit to the employees' retirement accounts using a predetermined formula and vesting schedule.

---

[44] Source: http://www.dol.gov/ebsa/mentalhealthparity/

Other Benefits

In addition to major health/welfare and retirement benefits, companies typically complement their benefits with paid time off, paid holidays, sick leave, and bereavement leave. Companies may also offer voluntary benefits to employees, such as critical illness coverage, long-term care coverage, wellness programs, automotive insurance, home insurance, and other coverage at a group discount. Offering a complete package of benefits to suit the various needs of employees helps attract well-qualified talent to the organization, and can be used as a retention tool as well.

Work-Life Balance Programs

As business demands continue to increase in the global economy, there is a risk of burnout with high performing employees. One way that organizations help manage burnout is by offering work-life balance programs, which seek to help employees integrate work and family life together through nontraditional work arrangements, counseling and support, and concierge services to employees. A common work-life benefit offered at companies is an **Employee Assistance Program**, which offers independent, confidential, and free counseling and support services for a range of issues including mental health, family life, financial concerns, legal issues, and other issues that are important to employees.

Companies with greater resources may also offer dry cleaning service, childcare referral services, on-site fitness centers, and other perks to help employees stay balanced. Additionally, flexible work schedules, job sharing, telecommuting, and compressed workweeks are additional programs that companies can offer to employees at a minimal cost. These programs can make it easier for employees to balance family needs while performing well on the job.

Recognition Programs

Recognition programs can have a significant impact on business performance and morale of employees. Some organizations have formal recognition programs with monetary rewards, while others offer informal or low-cost recognition programs. Regardless of budget, successful recognition programs share the following characteristics:

1. They reward results or behaviors, such as meeting sales targets, saving the company significant money, completing an important project, or otherwise affecting the business in a significantly positive way.

2. They provide feedback that is immediate and frequent. This creates a sense of positive reinforcement on positive, productive behaviors, and can be used as a motivational tool for achieving future success.

3. They offer opportunities for peer-to-peer recognition. This creates a positive team dynamic, camaraderie, and strong working relationships.

4. Recognition is done publicly and is embedded into the company's values. When employees are recognized publicly by leadership, it serves to help them feel appreciated and part of the company's success.

Having a culture of recognition is an important tool for retaining good employees and motivating new ones. When employees are able to celebrate their successes together, it helps to unite them toward a common goal and work better with each other.

FOCUS: MASLOW'S HIERARCHY OF NEEDS

According to psychologist Abraham Maslow, human beings have a range of needs ranging from the most basic (security) to the most complex (self-actualization). This theory is often represented in a pyramid, which shows the "steps" of needs each human being must reach toward psychological fulfillment[45].

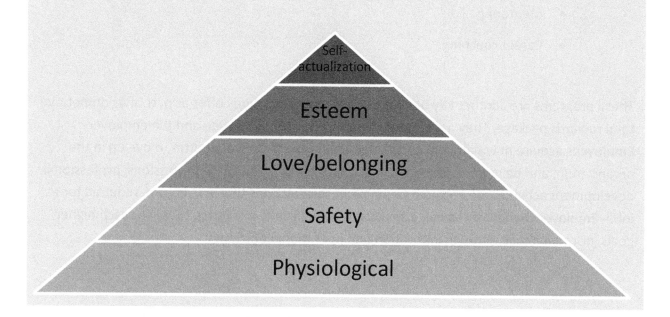

---

[45] Source: http://en.wikipedia.org/wiki/Maslow's_hierarchy_of_needs

According to Maslow's theory, two of the most valuable psychological needs humans have are the need to feel appreciated and the need to belong. Organizations can help meet these psychological needs through recognition programs, which can help employees feel appreciated, part of the organization, and valued. Having psychological needs met is an important element for an employee's decision to remain at the organization.

Professional Development Programs

Professional development refers to the acquisition of skills and knowledge, both for personal development and for career advancement. It can take the form of formalized training programs, external training opportunities, and financial assistance with work-related degree programs. Below are some examples of common professional development programs that companies offer to employees:

- Training seminars and workshops (internal)
- External seminars and workshops
- Tuition assistance for advanced (work-related) degrees
- Reimbursement for certification exams and recertification fees
- Mentoring
- Career coaching

These programs are another key benefit that many organizations offer as part of a competitive total rewards package. They are mutually beneficial to the employee and the employer. Employees acquire new skills and knowledge that make them work better, move up in the organization, and be more competitive in the marketplace. (In some professions, professional development activities are required to maintain certifications that are, in turn, required for a job.) Employers benefit by having a smarter, more efficient workforce that can reach higher goals, or reduce costs through innovation and operational efficiency.

Payroll

Payroll departments manage the payments, tax withholdings, and deductions of employees. Payroll administrators typical handle the following processes in order to ensure the proper and timely compensation of employees:

- Calculating time cards

- Calculating salaries, wages, reimbursements, commissions, bonuses, overtime, and retroactive pay

- Tracking and paying company paid holidays, vacation time, and sick time

- Handling paycheck deductions for taxes, wage garnishment, insurance, and retirement savings

- Coordinate with accounting/finance department to report all payments and deductions accurately

While human resources and payroll are considered two distinct functions, they often work hand-in-hand (and are sometimes combined in smaller organizations)[46]. For example, when HR initiates the hiring of an employee, payroll sets up the employee in the payroll system, collects and sets up the employee's tax withholdings and deductions, and adds the employee onto the roster for paycheck processing.

Smaller organizations may outsource their payroll and/or human resources duties to third-party administrators (TPA). A TPA can help the organization with administration of payroll, benefits, and HR records, often at a cost lower than hiring full-time staff. Other organizations, especially growing ones, employ an internal person (such as an office manager) to act as a liaison between employees and TPAs to ensure that issues are appropriately addressed and administration is handled timely and accurately. Even larger companies outsource all or part of their HR or payroll functions if it makes sense for the organization's budget, operations, and long-term goals.

Organizations often include both human resources and payroll management in the strategic planning process to ensure that their processes are closely aligned with the strategic goals of the organization. For example, human resources leadership can develop the appropriate strategies to attract, hire, and retain the best employees for the company. Payroll, meanwhile, can develop strategies to streamline processes, ensure high accuracy in recordkeeping, and

---

[46] Source: http://yourbusiness.azcentral.com/functions-payroll-vs-human-resource-7956.html

provide excellent service to employees. Both functions can work together to conduct (or assist in) internal audits to ensure the accuracy of employee records and employment practices such as paying employees.

Global Compensation

Designing, planning and managing employee compensation and benefits on a global basis can be challenging, especially when companies expand their operations into new regions while attempting to remain consistent with their total rewards philosophy. When offering compensation and benefits to international employees, companies need to be knowledgeable of the country or region's culture and regulations, which can have a direct impact on the types of compensation and benefit programs the company can offer to employees in a particular location.

Centralized Approach to Global Compensation

When organizations centralize their approach to global compensation, they create a centralized compensation structure that provides guidelines that are used for all positions in all locations, while maintaining a degree of flexibility to manage the unique needs and expectations of the workforce in various locations. Having a centralized system can have tangible benefits to the organization, including simplified financial planning, increased transparency in compensation practices, consistency in the enforcement of compensation practices, and reduced administrative expenses.

According to a September 2006 Watson Wyatt Worldwide survey of 275 companies with global operations, a majority plan to take a centralized approach to their global compensation structure[47]. Yet, many of these organizations also face ongoing challenges in implementing a centralized approach to compensation and benefits. Global companies must be able to manage variations in compensation structures due to economic factors, local customs that can dictate what compensation and benefits are expected of a population, and holiday schedules which can impact the organization's operations and compensation of employees.

Common Issues with Global Compensation

In order to remain compliant and consistent with international customs, laws, and regulations, companies must handle many issues surrounding the compensation of their global workforce:

---

[47] Source: http://talentmgt.com/articles/view/going_global_managing_the_challenges_of_global_compensation

- *Privacy and data regulations* – Regulations vary from country to country. Companies with employees in European Union countries must follow the *EU Data Protection Directive*, which sets restrictions on how personal information can be collected, stored and shared. The EU also restricts the sharing of data with countries that do not have rigorous security standards[48].

- *Maintaining pay equity* – Base pay and traditional compensation structures vary from country to country. For example, in France, base pay can include vacation pay and overtime payments. Regional differences must be factored in to the overall compensation program, and they must be accounted for when analyzing internal pay equity.

- *Accounting for cost of living* – The value of a US dollar in a given country affects the pay levels of employees in that country. For example, a $60,000 USD position in the US may pay $11,000 in India due to the difference in cost of living.

- *Managing cultural differences* – The way in which companies communicate with employees (especially with respect to their compensation and benefits) must be handled in accordance with the company's customs. For example, in China, employees expect their communications (e.g., employment agreements) to address them appropriately. To neglect doing so is considered offensive.

As organizations expand into international markets (or new countries), they must be prepared to address the issues with compensating their employees appropriately. As mentioned above, this process is often complex and requires knowledge of local laws, customs, and other factors. Companies should develop processes that make sense for their strategic plan, finances, and operations, while maintaining some flexibility to address differences. In some cases, the organization may decide to outsource its administrative payroll and HR functions for international employees in order to further manage the costs of operating abroad.

---

[48] Source: http://talentmgt.com/articles/view/going_global_managing_the_challenges_of_global_compensation/3

Main Ideas to Remember

→ "Total Rewards" describe all the tools an employer uses to attract, motivate, and retain employees. A total rewards package typically includes compensation, benefits, work/life programs, recognition programs, and professional development.

→ Employee compensation refers to the cash compensation that an employee receives in exchange for the work they perform. Typically, cash compensation consists of a wage or salary, and includes any commissions or bonuses.

→ Compensation can be categorized as fixed pay (base pay), variable pay (incentives/commissions), or premium pay (holiday/on-call/shift differential).

→ A company's pay structure is the method of administering its pay philosophy. The two most common types of pay structures are the internal equity method, which pays based on the job's placement in the organizational hierarchy, and market pricing, in which each job's pay is tied to the prevailing market rate.

→ To establish pay structures, HR conducts a process called compensation analysis, in which it analyzes its current payroll budget and trends; benchmarks a job's value using external data sources; determines the value of a job based on data and the organization's compensation philosophy; and creating salary ranges and pay grades.

→ The benefits that an organization offers to employees not only help the employees with their health, financial, and personal needs, but it can also make a total compensation package competitive and rich.

→ Employers are required by law to provide certain benefits to employees, including unemployment insurance, workers' compensation insurance, disability insurance, family and medical leave, and family military leave (depending on organization's size). The Affordable Care Act requires employers of certain sizes to provide health insurance to full time employees.

→ Health and welfare benefits are the most common discretionary benefits offered by employers. These benefits are typically offered in the form of a group health plan established or maintained by the employer (or union), and provides medical care for participants (and often their dependents) directly or through insurance, reimbursement, or otherwise.

→ A cafeteria plan (also called a Code section 125 plan or a flexible benefits plan) allows an employee to reduce his or her compensation in order to pay his or her share for employer-provided benefits coverage on a pre-tax basis.

→ Employee Retirement Income Security Act (ERISA) provides protections for participants and beneficiaries covered under employee benefit plans. Plan administrators and fiduciaries are required to meet certain standards of conduct that are outlined in the law.

→ Consolidated Omnibus Budget Reconciliation Act (COBRA) grants employees the right to pay premiums for and keep the group health insurance that they would otherwise lose after they quit or lose their jobs, or reduce their work hours. Most people can retain their insurance coverage for up to 18 months (and longer in some situations).

→ Health Insurance Portability and Accountability Act of 1996 (HIPAA) provides opportunities for people to retain (or obtain) health insurance during qualifying events; protects the confidentiality and security of healthcare information; and provides mechanisms to control administrative costs.

→ Americans with Disabilities Act requires that disabled and non-disabled individuals must be provided the same benefits, premiums, deductibles, and limits under a given health plan.

→ The Family and Medical Leave Act (FMLA) provides up to 12 weeks of job-protected, unpaid leave during any 12-month period to eligible, covered employees for the following reasons: 1) birth and care of the eligible employee's child, or placement for adoption or foster care of a child with the employee; 2) care of an immediate family member (spouse, child, parent) who has a serious health condition; or 3) care of the employee's own serious health condition. The law also requires that employee's group health benefits be maintained during the leave.

→ A retirement plan is a savings arrangement designed to replace employment income upon retirement. These plans may be set up by employers, unions, or other institutions. Retirement plans fall under three types of categories: defined benefit plan, defined contribution plan, and profit sharing plan.

→ In addition to major health/welfare and retirement benefits, companies typically complement their benefits with paid time off, paid holidays, sick leave, and bereavement leave. Companies may also offer voluntary benefits to employees, such as critical illness coverage, long-term care coverage, wellness programs, automotive insurance, home insurance, and other coverage at a group discount.

→ One way that organizations help manage burnout is by offering work-life balance programs, which seek to help employees integrate work and family life together through nontraditional work arrangements, counseling and support, and concierge services to employees. A common work-life benefit offered at companies is an Employee Assistance Program, which offers independent, confidential, and free counseling and support services for a range of issues including mental health, family life, financial concerns, legal issues, and other issues that are important to employees.

→ Having a culture of recognition is an important tool for retaining good employees and motivating new ones. When employees are able to celebrate their successes together, it helps to unite them toward a common goal and work better with each other.

→ Professional development refers to the acquisition of skills and knowledge, both for personal development and for career advancement. It can take the shape of formalized training programs, external training opportunities, and financial assistance with work-related degree programs.

→ The payroll function manages the payments, tax withholdings, and deductions of employees. Payroll administrators typical handle the following processes in order to ensure the proper and timely compensation of employees: calculating wages, reimbursements, deductions, and wage garnishments; tracking company paid holidays, vacation, and sick time; calculating time cards; and coordinating data with accounting/finance department.

→ Executive compensation differs from the package offered to lower-level employees. Executive compensation packages include base salary; bonus or incentives; stock options; income protection; severance; and exclusive insurance coverage.

→ When offering compensation and benefits to international employees, companies need to be knowledgeable of the country or region's culture and regulations, which can have a direct impact on the types of compensation and benefit programs the company can offer to employees in a particular location.

→ When organizations centralize their approach to global compensation, they create a centralized compensation structure that provides guidelines used for all positions in all locations, while maintaining a degree of flexibility to manage the unique needs and expectations of the workforce in various locations.

Key Terms to Review

Americans with Disabilities Act

Cafeteria Plan

COBRA

Compensation

Compensation analysis

Cost of living

Defined benefit plan

Defined contribution plan

Disability insurance

Employee benefits

ERISA

Executive compensation

Family and Medical Leave

Fixed pay

Flexible Spending Account

Health and welfare benefits

Health Reimbursement Account

Health Savings Account

HIPAA

Internal equity method

Mandated benefits

Market pricing

Maslow's hierarchy of needs

Mental Health Parity Act

Military Family Leave

Patient Protection and Affordable Care Act

Pay equity

Pay structures

Payroll

Pregnancy Discrimination Act

Premium pay

Professional development program

Profit sharing

Recognition program

Retirement plan

Social Security

Third-party administrator

Total rewards

Unemployment insurance

USERRA

Variable pay

Workers' compensation insurance

Work-life balance program

Training & Development

Section Overview

→ What is the importance of employee communications?

→ What forms of communication do organizations use?

→ What are the various ways employees can learn new concepts?

→ Why are training programs important?

→ What training techniques can be used on employees?

→ Why is feedback important? What types of feedback to managers give to employees?

→ How do managers evaluate performance?

→ What is the purpose of a performance appraisal, and how does it help employees as well as the organization?

Employee Communications

Employee communications are the methods that an organization uses to share knowledge with and obtain feedback from employees. The medium, manner, tone, and frequency of communications with employees are important for the success of the organization and the motivation of its people. When people have regular and open access to information, and can ask questions and provide feedback, they can more easily align themselves with the goals, strategies, and objectives of the organization, department, or team. Employee communications can be organization-wide (macro level) or employee-specific (micro level). They can take many forms including:

- Announcement of new product or service

- Information about companywide benefits and open enrollment

- Disclosure of company quarterly earnings

- Announcement of business changes

- Formal and informal feedback

- Invitation to companywide event

- Explanation of a new process

Using a combination of media for conveying information across the organization can be effective for reaching employees in multiple locations, with different schedules, or even with different learning styles. Below are some examples of media used:

- Email messages

- Bulletin board

- Company intranet

- Company newsletters

- Companywide halls

- Team or department meetings

- Conference calls

- One-on-one conversations

- Training sessions

The messages should be tailored to be appropriate for the media used as well as the audience (i.e., the whole company or a specific group of employees). It is important, as well, to maintain open lines of communication in order to maintain transparency with employees and ensure that the messages are conveyed and understood by employees. There should also be mechanisms for information to flow upward (from employees to leadership) as well as downward, so that information is freely exchanged between leadership and staff[49].

A company and employees can benefit from effective employee communications in many ways:

- Roles in the organization are clarified and employees can understand how they contribute to the "bottom line" or mission.

- Employees can understand changes in the organization more clearly, ask questions, and gain more information that is useful for them to adapt to change. This helps reduce anxiety, which can lead to lower productivity or higher turnover among staff.

- Customer service is improved when employees fully understand the product or service, and understand what is expected of them in their roles.

- Leadership can gain valuable input from staff on products/services, operations, or other items that can help advance the organization's mission.

- Consistent and open communications establish trust in the organization and help to encourage loyalty to the organization. Being upfront and honest can help dispel rumors in the organization and encourage employees to ask questions.

It is important for leadership to communicate information regularly to staff, and to solicit feedback in return. When feedback is received, it is important for leadership to be responsive toward it and address the feedback whenever possible. Having a two-way communication will keep a dialogue going, establish trust, and generate new ideas. Companies should establish a communications plan when undergoing change, especially in order to ensure that the message is fully understood by all key constituents.

---

[49] Source: https://www.go2hr.ca/articles/speak-easy-importance-ongoing-employee-communications

Training and Learning

As mentioned in the last section, it is important for employee communications to be presented in multiple ways because adults all have different learning styles. By communicating to various learning styles, the organization is likely to minimize confusion and be more confident that the message is conveyed by all staff.

Learning styles refer to the method people best learn a new concept. Some people prefer to see a message, others prefer to hear it, and some people learn by doing something. Some people prefer a combination of learning styles, too. While there is no "right" or "wrong" way to learn, it is important for organizational leadership and human resources to understand the various adult learning styles:

Types of Learning Styles

- Visual (spatial): Learn through pictures, drawings, and images.

- Aural (auditory-musical): Learn through sound or music.

- Verbal (linguistic): Learn through words (verbal and writing)

- Physical (kinesthetic): Learn through touch or movement.

- Logical (mathematical): Learn through logic or reasoning.

Granted, it is not always practical to tailor a message or concept to every learning style. It is important, though, for organizational leaders, trainers, and HR professionals to understand that everyone processes and learns new information in different ways. Therefore, when explaining concepts to employees, organizations should strive to use a combination of methods and media that are appropriate for the particular message and the available resources.

Training Programs & Techniques

Employee training programs are important for educating staff, preparing them to perform a job, and helping them acquire valuable skills that are relevant to the job. In other words, training helps employees acquire the tools, strategies, and techniques necessary to be successful at their jobs. There is a variety of methods that an organization can use to train employees, which fall into two categories: cognitive and behavioral. Each has their own advantages and disadvantages, and is appropriate depending on the learning styles of employees.

Cognitive Methods

Cognitive methods of training are based on theoretical training that focuses on processes, guidelines, methods, and rules. Information is provided either in verbal or written form and results in increased knowledge or change of mindset. Examples of cognitive-based training include:

- Live demonstrations and tutorials
- Lectures to provide information
- Group discussions for process-based problem solving
- Computer or web-based training

Behavioral Methods

Behavioral methods of training are interactive and intended to spark creative thinking. They focus on employee behaviors and problem solving rather than processes. Examples of behavioral training include:

- Role playing with open ended problem solving
- Behavior modeling ("show and tell") to compare scenarios
- Case studies with open discussion about outcomes
- Group brainstorming to solve sample problems

Both methods have their advantages and disadvantages. Cognitive training can be useful for providing consistency, but lacks in encouraging creative thinking. Behavioral methods challenge trainees to develop their own solutions but does not provide for uniformity. Knowing the advantages and disadvantages of each, along with the desired outcomes of the training will help the organization determine which type of training to utilize. In addition, although these two methods of training are the most commonly used, there are other effective methods to train employees, including one-on-one coaching/mentoring, soft skills training, and formal and informal feedback[50].

---

[50] Source: http://employeetraininghq.com/methods-of-training-employees/

Employee Feedback and Performance Appraisal

Feedback is arguably one of the most important duties of managers, and is critical for an employee's success. HR practitioners have a key role in collaborating with management to ensure that feedback is timely, consistent, and impactful. Feedback can be formal (i.e. performance reviews; write-ups) or they can be informal (i.e. conversations, meetings).

Informal Feedback

Informal feedback is instant, in-the-moment advice that occurs outside the formal performance review (which occurs typically once a year). Informal feedback can be given to praise an employee for accomplishing a goal, correcting a mistake, or providing constructive criticism to be used going forward. Feedback should be specific, using data or examples, and it should be immediate so that the situation is fresh on the employee's mind. Providing feedback can help good employees sustain their success, and coach poor or average performing employees to take immediate steps to improve. Managers can and should provide feedback to employees in the following situations:

Situations for positive reinforcement:

- When an employee demonstrates improvement in a development area
- When an employee goes "above and beyond" their job
- When an employee "pitches in" to help colleagues
- When an employee reaches an important goal or milestone
- When an employee sets a good example for others

Situations for constructive criticism:

- When an employee is not performing the job correctly and is making mistakes
- When an employee is being disruptive to the team or not following rules
- When an employee is not meeting the expectations of the job
- When an employee needs to develop a particular skill

Employees usually perform better when they receive timely and specific feedback from their managers. Sometimes employees are not aware that their performance is an issue or that they are doing something wrong (or in other cases, that they are doing well). Feedback provides them with specific information they need about the manager's expectations, so they can correct their behavior (when receiving constructive feedback) or continue on the same path (when receiving praise). When the employee's behavior changes (whether positively or negatively), it is important for the manager to follow up and give new feedback as necessary.

Performance Appraisals

In addition to informal feedback, described in the previous section, formal feedback is an important activity to support the success of the organization's workforce. The most common type of formal feedback is the performance appraisal, which is a documented assessment of the employee's performance in a specific period of time (typically a year) that contributes to the employee's overall development.

According the Society for Human Resource Management (SHRM), performance appraisals complement the organization's strategic plan, which determines individual job tasks and requirements. The appraisal is based on results achieved by the employee in his/her job, rather than his/her personal characteristics. It measures skills and accomplishments with reasonable accuracy and uniformity, often using a predetermined scale, rubric, and criteria. The evaluation should be conducted using specific data, examples, and feedback from colleagues or customers. Done thoroughly, the appraisal provides a way to help identify areas for improving performance and helping the employee to grow professionally.

Periodic reviews help managers stay in tune with their employees' abilities, set a clear path moving forward, and help their teams work more effectively. Performance appraisals should recognize the employees' achievement, evaluate their progress and identify ways for improving or expanding their skills. If the manager has been providing ongoing and specific feedback during the year, the performance appraisal should not provide many surprises to the employee. The appraisal, then, serves as a tool for documenting the employee's progress and facilitates the accompanying conversation the employee has with his/her manager. Typically, the appraisal is signed by both the manager and employee to confirm receipt of the document and/or confirm the performance conversation.

Appraisals are also tools for managing organizational risk. Sometimes these documents are requested during litigation or hearings with governmental agencies (for unemployment or discrimination claims). Organizations that have thorough, timely, and relevant performance appraisals documented in the employee's file can respond to complaints more effectively. If an organization does not document performance appraisals, or does appraisals inconsistently, it can be a risk to the organization. A licensed employment attorney can help employers understand their particular risk and respond to complaints if they arise.

Review

Main Ideas to Remember

→ Employee communications are all the methods that an organization uses to share knowledge with and obtain feedback from employees. When people have regular and open access to information, and can ask questions and provide feedback, they can more easily align themselves with the goals, strategies, and objectives of the organization, department, or team.

→ Using a combination of media for conveying information across the organization can be effective for reaching employees in multiple locations, with different schedules, or even with different learning styles. The messages should be tailored to be appropriate for the media used as well as the audience (i.e., the whole company or a specific group of employees). There should also be mechanisms for information to flow upward (from employees to leadership) as well as downward, so that information is freely exchanged between leadership and staff

→ *Learning styles* refer to the method people best learn a new concept. Some people prefer to see a message, others prefer to hear it, and some people learn by doing something. Some people prefer a combination of learning styles, too.

→ Adult learning styles are visual, aural, verbal, physical, and logical. While there is no "right" or "wrong" way to learn, it is important for organizational leadership and human resources to understand the various learning styles of adults.

→ Employee training programs are important for educating staff, preparing them to perform a job, and helping them acquire valuable skills that are relevant to the job. In other words, training helps employees acquire the tools, strategies, and techniques necessary to be successful at their jobs.

→ There are a variety of methods that an organization can use to train employees, which fall into two categories: cognitive (process driven) and behavioral (interactive). Each has their own advantages and disadvantages, and is appropriate depending on the learning styles of employees.

→ *Informal feedback* is instant, in-the-moment advice that occurs outside the formal performance review (which occurs typically once a year). Informal feedback can be given to praise an employee for accomplishing a goal, correcting a mistake, or providing constructive criticism to be used going forward.

→ Employees usually perform better when they receive timely and specific feedback from their managers. Sometimes employees are not aware that their performance is an issue or that they are doing something wrong (or in other cases, that they are doing well). Feedback provides them with specific information they need about the manager's expectations, so that they can correct their behavior (when receiving constructive feedback) or continue on the same path (when receiving praise).

→ The most common type of formal feedback is the performance appraisal, which is a documented assessment of the employee's performance in a specific period of time (typically a year) that contributes to the employee's overall development. Performance appraisals should recognize the employees' achievement, evaluate their progress, and identify ways for improving or expanding their skills.

Key Terms to Review

Adult learning styles

Behavioral method of training

Cognitive method of training

Communications medium

Constructive criticism

Employee communications

Informal feedback

Performance appraisal

Rating scale

Employee & Labor Relations

Section Overview

→ What is the role of employee relations in an organization?

→ What methods do manager use to maintain employee relations?

→ What is the significance of organizational culture?

→ What major federal laws must employers comply with?

→ What special obligations or requirements do recipients of federal government contracts, grants, or aid have?

→ What laws affect specific industries?

→ What is the purpose of an employee handbook?

→ What information is typically included in an employee handbook?

→ What protections do union and non-union employees have?

→ How has the National Labor Relations Act changed labor relations? How has the scope of the law changed over time?

→ How does an employee complaint differ from a grievance? How is it similar? Why are both important to employees and management?

→ What are the steps of progressive discipline?

→ How are employee relations and labor relations handled in a global environment?

Employee Relations

Employee relations is the maintenance of employer-employee relationships to maintain high productivity and morale. When conducted effectively, it improves the understanding of the organization's policies, procedures, and expectations to employees. People who handle employee relations deal with conflict, poor behavior, and difficult situations – and identify ways to both prevent and resolve those types of issues through special programs and communications. Employee handbooks (described elsewhere in this guide) are an important tool for maintaining sound employee relations through the consistent and fair treatment of employees, as well as clear written expectations. Handbooks and written policies are a key method for documenting expectations and practices such as fair hiring and equal employment opportunity.

HR professionals perform employee relations when they advise managers on how to manage poor performance or handle employee misconduct. When an employee violates a policy that is documented in the handbook, for example, the manager or HR professional can reference that policy and enforce it equitably. In these situations, a manager may decide to coach the employee or take disciplinary actions that are appropriate to the situation. When an employee complains about his/her work conditions or supervisor, HR often takes an active role to investigate the situation, interview witnesses, and make recommendations for appropriate action. Often a degree of interpretation is needed, as not all situations are expressly documented in a policy. Management or HR will need to interpret a policy, when situations are not clear-cut, and take action (or make recommendations for action) based on the facts and the policy's application to the situation.

The employee's manager or department may have his or her own specific procedures and expectations that are typically aligned with those of the overall organization. When employees are not performing well or behave in an unacceptable manner, the manager will counsel the employee, identify the issues, and discuss a plan to correct the problem. When an employee files a complaint about his or her work conditions, management or HR will discuss the concerns, investigate if necessary, and collect key data to make an informed decision. In serious situations such as sexual harassment or discrimination, employees are typically reminded of their grievance and appeal rights and discrimination, as well as any whistleblower protections. When these situations are handled, they are often documented in the employee's file or another record repository for future reference or required government reporting.

A major benefit of sound employee relations is the ability of the organization to maintain open, productive relationships between employees and management. By proactively identifying issues and being responsive to complaints or problems, organizations can thwart or diminish disruptive behavior. Having managers actively helping to manage employee relations and act as problem solvers is key to a successful partnership. When employees are aware of their developmental areas and have the support and resources they need to improve, it benefits both the employees and the organization.

Organizational Culture

Organizational culture is the workplace environment that is fostered by both leadership and employees. At its very essence, it describes how people within the organization interact with one another, and it is affected by the experiences, personalities, values, beliefs, and principles of leadership and employees. Everyone within the organization contributes to the organizational culture in some way, and every organization has its own unique culture. Culture is often a reason why employees may decide to remain at an organization, or leave the organization. It can also affect the organization's success.

An organization's culture affects its overall identity, the way that employees, clients, and the general public view the organization. For this reason, many organizations take great care to articulate and instill its values in everything it does, so that it develops a strong reputation. When an organization is highly regarded for its reputation, it helps attract strong candidates to work there and clients to purchase its products or services. A shared organizational culture helps to keep the workforce cohesive, especially when many employees come from different backgrounds, geographies, and cultures. When they feel a sense of unity through culture, and they feel that they work in a supportive environment with strong values, they are more likely to communicate more effectively, work more collaboratively, and have conflicts less frequently.

Organizational culture is also a motivational tool. When employees feel connected to the organization and understand the significance of their role, they are more likely to feel invested in the organization's success. When they feel they have a stake in the success of the organization, they are more likely to work harder to accomplish the organization's goals. Having clear expectations and objectives set by management can help each employee understand his or her roles and responsibilities. This strategic management, combined with a system of recognition and feedback, helps keep employees aligned with the objectives of the business unit and organization. Employees will perform at their personal best to earn recognition and appreciation from management, and the organization will benefit from greater productivity and cooperation.

Labor Laws

The U.S. Department of Labor (DOL) administers and enforces more than 180 federal laws. These mandates and the regulations that implement them cover many workplace activities for many organizations that employee people. Some laws cover certain types of employers; and some cover certain sizes. Employers are required to understand and comply with these laws as applicable[51].

Wage & Hour Law

The **Fair Labor Standards Act (FLSA)** mandates standards for the payment of regular wages and overtime, which affect most private and public employers. Employers are required to pay covered employees (i.e. non-exempt) at least the federal minimum wage and overtime pay of 1-1/2 times the regular rate of pay (time and a half). Children under 16 can only work certain hours, and children under 18 cannot work in dangerous non-agricultural jobs.

Garnishment of Wages

Employee wage garnishments are regulated under the Consumer Credit Protection Act (CPCA).

Workplace Safety & Health

The **Occupational Safety and Health Act** regulates the safety and health of employees, and is administered by the Occupational Safety and Health Administration (OSHA) who may conduct inspections and investigations. Employers covered by the Act must comply with the regulations and the safety and health standards set forth by OSHA. Employers also have a responsibility to provide their employees with work environment free from recognized, serious hazards.

Health Insurance

The Patient Protection and Affordable Care Act requires covered employers to provide affordable health insurance that provides minimum value to their full-time employees (and their dependents), to communicate about health-care marketplaces to employees, and to

---

[51] Source: http://www.dol.gov/opa/aboutdol/lawsprog.htm

provide a standardized summary of coverage to employees (among other requirements); requires insurers to cover pre-existing conditions and cover all insurance applicants. (Note: Many other components to the PPACA are not listed here. Check with the U.S. Department of Health and Human Services for complete information.)

Employee Benefit Security

The Employee Retirement Income Security Act (ERISA) regulates employers who offer pension or welfare benefit plans to their employees. The Act mandates a wide range of fiduciary, disclosure and reporting requirements on plan fiduciaries and those administering these plans. These provisions preempt (override) many similar state laws. Under Title IV of ERISA, certain employers and plan administrators must fund an insurance system to protect certain kinds of retirement benefits, with premiums paid to the federal government's Pension Benefit Guaranty Corporation (PBGC).

Health Insurance Continuation and Privacy

The Consolidated Omnibus Budget Reconciliation Act (COBRA) grants employees the right to pay premiums for and keep the group health insurance that they would otherwise lose after they quit or lose their jobs, or reduce their work hours. Most people can retain their insurance coverage for up to 18 months (and longer in some situations). The Health Insurance Portability and Accountability Act of 1996 (HIPAA) provides opportunities for people to retain (or obtain) health insurance during qualifying events; protects the confidentiality and security of healthcare information; and provides mechanisms to control administrative costs.

Family and Medical Leave

The **Family and Medical Leave Act (FMLA)** provides up to 12 weeks of job-protected, unpaid leave during any 12-month period to eligible, covered employees for the following reasons:

1) birth and care of the eligible employee's child, or placement for adoption or foster care of a child with the employee;

2) care of an immediate family member (spouse, child, parent) who has a serious health condition; or

3) care of the employee's own serious health condition.

The law also requires that employee's group health benefits be maintained during the leave. The FMLA was amended in 2008 to provide protections specifically for military families. For eligible, covered employees, up to 26 weeks of military caregiver leave (to care for injured family members), and up to 12 weeks of qualifying exigency leave (to tend to matters related to deployment). These leaves are also unpaid; however, the employee's group health benefits must be maintained during the leave.

Uniformed Services Employment and Reemployment Rights Act

Under USERRA, certain employees who serve in the armed forces have a right to reemployment with the employer they were with when they entered service, including reserves and National Guard.

Employee Polygraph Protection Act

This Act prohibits most employers from using lie detectors on employees, and permits polygraph tests only in limited circumstances.

Whistleblower Protection

Many labor-related, public safety and environmental laws protect whistleblowers—in general, employees who make good faith complaints about violations of the law committed by their employers. Penalties for violating these protections can include job reinstatement and payment of back wages. OSHA enforces the whistleblower protections in most cases.

Notification of Layoffs or Plant Closings

Mass layoffs or plant closings may be subject to the Worker Adjustment and Retraining Notification Act (WARN). WARN requires that employees receive early warning of impending layoffs or plant closings.

Special Requirements for Government Contractors

Recipients of government contracts, grants or financial aid are subject to their own set of wage, hour, benefits, and safety and health standards under the following laws:

- *Davis-Bacon Act* requires payment of prevailing wages and benefits to employees of contractors working in federal government construction projects

- *McNamara-O'Hara Service Contract Act* establishes wage rates and other work standards for employees of contractors providing services to the federal government

- *Walsh-Healey Public Contracts Act* requires payment of minimum wages and other work standards by contractors providing materials and goods to the federal government.

Government contractors are also required to comply with federal affirmative action and equal opportunity laws, executive orders, and regulations. The Office of Federal Contract Compliance Programs (OFCCP) administers and enforces these laws.

Industry-Specific Laws and Regulations

Several federal laws and regulations affect employers in the construction, agricultural, and mining industries.

- OSHA promulgates specific safety and health regulations for construction industry employers.

- The Migrant and Seasonal Agricultural Worker Protection Act (MSPA) regulates the employment of agricultural workers.

- The Fair Labor Standards Act (FLSA) exempts agricultural workers from overtime premium pay, but requires minimum wage for workers employed on larger farms. The Act has special regulations that prohibit children under 16 from working during school hours and in certain jobs deemed too dangerous.

- The Federal Mine Safety and Health Act of 1977 (Mine Act) mandates the safety and health standards of miners, as well as training of miners; levies penalties for violations; and allows inspectors to close dangerous mines.

State Laws and Regulations

The laws and regulations mentioned in this section are prescribed by the federal government. Individual states (and sometimes localities) create and enforce their own laws related to the employment of workers. Employers should be aware of the employment laws in all states in which they conduct business and have employees; the state's Department of Labor can be contacted for information about employment laws in that particular state. Employment practices and policies should be consistent with all laws that affect the organization in order to remain compliant and avoid penalties.

Company Policies & Handbooks

An **employee handbook**, also referred to as an *employee manual*, is a document of the organization's policies and procedures that affect all employees. It can provide both employment and practical information such as company rules, performance expectations, and office operations. A written employee handbook gives clear guidance to employees, sets expectations and creates a culture where issues are dealt with fairly and consistently[52]. It also outlines the organization's legal obligations as an employer, as well as employees' rights.

Sections and Policies in Handbooks

- *General Employment Information* - overview of the business and general employment policies, including employment eligibility, job classifications, employee records, probationary periods, performance reviews, termination procedures, company transfers and union information, if applicable.

- *Anti-Discrimination Policies* – information about how the company complies with equal opportunity, anti-harassment, non-discrimination, and disability laws. Includes procedures for complaints and grievances.

- *Standards of Conduct* – sets expectations of how employees should conduct themselves, including dress code and behavior in the workplace.

- *Conflict of Interest Statements* - helps to protect the company's trade secrets and proprietary information.

- *Payroll Procedures* – outlines pay schedules, timekeeping requirements, overtime pay, salary increases, bonuses, and deductions for taxes and benefit premiums.

- *Work Schedules* – explains work hours and schedules, attendance, punctuality and reporting absences.

- *Safety and Security* – explains employee's rights and obligations with creating a safe and secure workplace. Provides instructions on reporting accidents, injuries, and safety hazards. Provides guidance for securing files, computers, and other company resources.

- *Use of Computers and Technology* – describes the appropriate use of company-provided hardware and software; steps to keep data secure; and how to handle personally identifiable information. Typically states that there should be no expectation of privacy

---

[52] Source: http://en.wikipedia.org/wiki/Employee_handbook

for employees; the company owns the technology and may monitor and regulate its use.

- *Employee Benefits* – outlines any benefit programs and eligibility requirements, including all benefits that are required by law.

- *Time Off Policies* – when applicable, outlines the employees' entitlement for vacation time, sick time, paid holidays, family and medical leave, jury duty, military leave, and time off voting should all be documented to comply with state and local laws.

Many handbooks also contain specific language that invokes the doctrine of **employment at will**. An *"employment-at-will" statement* specifies that an employee or employer may terminate the employment relationship, with or without reason, and with or without notice. In an at-will employment situation (which is the case in many states), there is no expectation of employment either indefinitely or for a specified duration.

New employees are typically required to sign an acknowledgement form stating they have read and understand the information contained in the handbook. From time to time, the company may need to make updates to the handbook due to new policies, practices, and laws. Revisions should be communicated and distributed to employees and may require a new signed acknowledgment. Additionally, there may be different versions of the employee handbook for certain business units, subsidiaries, or locations. It is important to ensure that all versions are kept up to date.

Handbooks can be a useful tool in situations when corrective action needs to be taken on an employee, up to and including termination of employment. When writing up employees or terminating them, it is helpful to refer to the specific policy or policies being violated. Doing so not only makes it clear to the employee that corrective action has been taken for an objective reason (i.e. violating an established policy), but it is also useful for the company to reference when defending itself in litigation or complaints to governmental agencies. For this reason, a qualified employment attorney should review the company's handbook for compliance with the law and can provide counsel when the company needs to defend itself.

Labor Relations

The term *labor relations* describes the interaction between employers and employees, typically in a unionized environment. (However, in some cases it applies to non-union workers as well.) Labor relations also examine how employees are affected by economic factors including globalization and recession, and this process seeks to find ways to minimize negative impact on the workforce. When labor relations are strong at an organization, management works effectively with employee representatives (typically labor unions) to solve problems in ways that are both in the interest of the employee and the organization. For example, if the cost of materials rises substantially and threatens mass layoffs, the labor relations process could find ways to cut costs elsewhere, find new ways to adapt to the changes, and innovate new products or strategies for the business that are sustainable.

Labor relations are regulated by the U.S. government, which provides guidance on the treatment of employees. A major law governing labor relations in the United States is the **National Labor Relations Act of 1935** (also called the **Wagner Act**), which is enforced by the National Labor Relations Board. This act granted most *private-sector* workers a large number of labor rights, including the right to strike, to bargain as a union, and to protest the conditions of their employment. (It does not apply to management, governmental employees, independent contractors, and certain other employees as outlined in the statute.) Employees covered by the Wagner Act are granted certain rights to join together to improve their wages and working conditions, with or without a union. This means that although a union may not be present in an organization, employees at that organization still have rights to talk about the conditions of their employment with one another and take action as a group, as discussed below.

FOCUS: Union Activity

Under the National Labor Relations Act, employees have the right to attempt to form a union where one does not currently exist, and to decertify a union that employees no longer support. In exchange for membership dues, the union represents employees on matters related to their pay, benefits, and workplace conditions. The union will assist employees when they file complaints or grievances, or when an employer is not abiding by a collective bargaining agreement. Employers are prohibited by federal law from retaliating against employees who form a union or engage in protected activity covered under the NLRA.

The NLRA also protects employees who are not represented by a union but are engaged in "concerted activity." **Concerted activity** occurs when two or more employees take action for their mutual benefit or protection with respect to the conditions or terms of their employment. For example, concerted activity may include a group of employees approaching a manager to raise their wages. It may also apply to two or more employees speaking to each other about work-related issues such as safety concerns. A single employee may also engage in a concerted activity if he or she acts on behalf of a group of employees, raises complaints on behalf of a group of employees, or tries to coordinate a group to take action.

The effects of the NLRA were changed substantially when the Taft-Hartley Act was passed in 1947. Taft-Hartley outlawed closed shops, jurisdictional strikes, and secondary boycotts. It set up mechanisms for decertifying unions and allowed states to pass certain anti-union legislation such as right-to-work laws. Additionally, under the law, employers and unions are forbidden to contribute funds out of their treasuries to candidates for federal office; management is not afforded union protection; and the unions seeking the services of the National Labor Relations Board have to file documents with the U.S. Department of Labor.

While the National Labor Relations Act and Taft-Hartley are the most well-known laws involving labor relations, a large amount of legislation can be accurately described as labor relations. Minimum wage laws, fair-practice rules, wage theft laws, and legislation mandating danger pay are all examples of laws that were passed because of influence from organized labor.

Words to Know

Agency shop: A union security clause that requires all union members and non-union employees to pay a service fee (similar to dues).

Arbitration: The referral of disputes to an impartial third party (an arbitrator, as opposed to court). The arbitrator's decision is typically final and binding.

Bargaining unit: A group of employees who bargain collectively with their employer (i.e. through a union).

Closed shop: The practice of employing only union members. Made illegal under the Taft-Hartley Act.

Collective bargaining: A negotiation process between the union and employer about wages and other conditions of employment.

Executive Order 10988: Allows federal employees to collectively bargain with management; signed by President John F. Kennedy.

Lockout: The act of an employer closing a facility to coerce workers to meet a demand.

Open shop: The practice of employing people without respect to union membership.

Picketing: The public protest of an employer by workers, and the discouragement of non-striking workers and customers to enter the business. Typically takes place during a strike (when the bargaining unit refuses to work until a collective bargaining agreement is made.)

Right-to-work law: Prohibits or limits union agreements that require employees' membership, or payment of union dues or fees, as a condition of employment. Despite what they are called, these laws do not provide a general guarantee of employment.

Seniority: A worker's length of service with an employer. In union contracts, seniority often determines layoffs from work and recalls back to work.

Taft-Hartley Act: Limited the reach and influence of the NLRA. Outlawed the closed shop and certain strike and boycott activity. Allows states to pass right-to-work laws and sets up mechanisms for decertifying unions. Limited who is covered under NLRA and provided stricter rules for unions seeking the assistance of the National Labor Relations Board.

Unfair labor practices: Under NLRA and Taft-Hartley, is defined as discrimination, coercion, and intimidation prohibited to labor and management. For example, management cannot form company unions or use coercive tactics to discourage union organization. Likewise, unions cannot force workers to join.

Union security clause: A clause in the collective bargaining agreement that provides for a union shop, maintenance of membership, or an agency shop.

Union shop: A shop where every member of the bargaining unit is required to join the union after a specified amount of time.

Dispute Resolution

A major activity in employee relations is the management of employee complaints and grievances. Complaints are generally less serious or severe than grievances, but both require timely and thoughtful action.

Complaints

Employee complaints can range in topics from the type of coffee provided to the management style of one's boss. Some complaints are quickly and easily resolved by management or HR, while other complaints require more time, effort, and patience. Even if you consider employee complaints to be a nuisance, they can provide HR and management with useful information. They can alert management of a problem before it grows out of control, and give management a chance to respond and show its commitment to addressing employee concerns.

When a manager or HR professional is presented with a complaint, he or she should listen carefully and openly to identify the concern behind the complaint. Asking pointed questions to gather facts will help decide a proper plan of action. If it seems that this concern is shared with other employees, talking to other employees to obtain their perspective can be useful for identifying widespread issues. During this process, it is important to acknowledge the problem and identify what appropriate action is being taken. If action is not being taken on the complaint, it is appropriate to explain why. Demonstrating follow-through is essential to maintaining employee trust.

While complaints are inevitable, there are methods that can be used to minimize employee complaints. HR professionals can encourage managers to give ongoing feedback on performance and set clear expectations for the role. Employees can be encouraged to have a reasonable amount of input in their work, and give their opinions on specific topics. (However, this should be done with care as not to encourage more complaining.) Granted, not every employee is going to be satisfied with every action taken in an organization, and some employees may seem to be never satisfied. It is important not to penalize legitimate complainants. If you do, the employer may silence this valuable source of information. Instead, if someone is making petty complaints on a regular basis, it is essential to have a matter-of-fact conversation as to how the complaining is harming the morale of the organization (if it is) and explain that the *manner* in which he/she is complaining is unacceptable.

Grievances

Grievances, on the other hand, are formal complaints made by employees when they believe a company policy, a collective bargaining agreement, or a law, has been violated. Grievances are red flags warning HR and management about large problems that require immediate attention. Even more than complaints, it is essential to respond swiftly to grievances[53]. A prompt response that results in a quick resolution of the grievance will improve employee morale and productivity, and can potentially prevent costly legal action.

Responding to Grievances

It is imperative to take all grievances seriously, even if they may not seem valid on the surface. HR can test the validity of a grievance by obtaining all relevant facts, as follows:

1. Actively listen to the person with the grievance. Ask follow up questions and get concrete examples, dates, times, witnesses, and other alleged facts.

2. Consult with an employment attorney or union steward. It is important that careful steps be taken when validating a grievance. In unionized environments, the collective bargaining agreement may have specific steps outlined.

3. Interview potential witnesses, as appropriate, to obtain their perspective of the situation.

4. Provide an update to the person who submitted the grievance. If it seems that there is a problem that needs further investigation or action, specify what will be done. If the grievance does not seem valid, explain what was done up to this point, and why no further action will be taken.

5. If it is valid, take action to rectify the situation.

Taking Action on Grievances

1. If the organization has a collective bargaining agreement, follow the guidelines within it for handling grievances (and with the assistance of a union steward). Otherwise, refer to the employee handbook if there is a specific policy or procedure outlined.

2. Complainants and their supervisors should try to resolve the problem through discussion, which may be facilitated by HR.

---

[53] Source: http://edwardlowe.org/digital-library/handling-complaints-and-grievances/

3. If no resolution is met, the next higher level of management may speak with the employee, without repercussions. Again, this may also be facilitated by HR.

4. During any part of this process, HR may take a more active approach as a mediator. In some cases, however, a third-party arbitrator (outside of the organization) may be used.

There are steps an organization can take to minimize their risk of employee grievances. It is important to stay in touch with employees and be open to feedback. There should be a system in place where employees can file legitimate complaints before they become bigger and unmanageable. Having a clear policy or procedure on submitting grievances, and detailing how the employer will handle grievances, will promote open communication. When employees complain, it is important not to retaliate against them simply for making a complaint. While not every complaint may be acted upon, it is important to acknowledge the concerns and feelings of employees and be clear on what action will or will not be taken, and the reasons behind those decisions.

Employee Discipline & Terminations

Most employees strive to do well at their jobs, but sometimes they do not meet the expectations of the job or exhibit behaviors that are unacceptable. When this happens, most managers use an approach called progressive discipline, a series of steps that offer opportunities to improve. If the employee does not improve during one step, then he or she progresses to the next step, which is considered more severe and moves closer to termination[54].

The Steps of Progressive Discipline

The number and details of each step in progressive discipline vary from employer to employer. Some employers, especially those subject to collective bargaining agreements, require a strict use of each step in succession. Others, however, reserve the right to use any or all steps necessary to address a particular issue. For example, not following the company's dress code may subject an employee to a verbal warning, but physical violence toward another employee will likely result in immediate termination. Taking steps of progressive discipline is typically useful for non-serious offenses that are repetitive, or where there is no indication of improvement by the employee. Below are typical steps found in a progressive discipline procedure.

Chart: A typical progressive discipline procedure

| Verbal Warning | Written Warning | Probation or Suspension | Termination |

---

[54] Source: http://everydaylife.globalpost.com/types-discipline-used-workplace-2647.html

Verbal Warning

A verbal warning is the least serious consequence of a poor behavior. It involves a conversation between a supervisor an employee, in which the inappropriate behavior is identified and expectations for improvement are made clear.

Written Warning

A written warning is appropriate when the employee ignores a verbal warning about his or her behavior or does not show improvement. The "write-up" documents the incident, explains why the behavior is inappropriate (and references applicable company policies), tells what needs to change, and describes the consequences of the continued behavior. Typically, an employee is asked to sign a copy to acknowledge receipt, although a signature may not necessarily mean the employee agrees with the contents of the write-up.

Performance Improvement Plan

A performance improvement plan places the employee on probation and requires specific actions to be taken in order to meet the supervisor's expectations. The employee is required to follow the plan, and show improvement, as a condition of continued employment.

Suspension

A suspension, if used, is often the final step before termination. A suspension lasts a certain duration, may be paid or unpaid, and is accompanied by a document that outlines the terms of the suspension, specific steps that need to be taken to correct the issue, and the consequences for not improving. When the employee completes the suspension, he or she typically receives one last chance to demonstrate improvement.

Termination

Termination of employment (or firing) is the final step in the progressive discipline process when behavioral problems are continual, or the employee commits gross misconduct such as theft or violence. Usually a firing is immediate, but should not be a surprise if the employer has clearly conveyed expectations and provided ongoing feedback to the employee.

There are other steps for progressive discipline that may be used, including demotions, temporary pay cuts, reassignments, and required training. Whatever methods are used, they should fit the behavior and seek to resolve the problem rather than simply provide a route toward termination. Being open and frank during each step of the process can help the employee improve.

Focus: Weingarten Rights

Unionized workplaces offer specific protections to employees during progressive discipline. Under the Weingarten Rights doctrine, named for the Supreme Court ruling of *NLRB v. J. Weingarten, Inc.,* an employee has the right to request union representation when they are investigated or being disciplined. An employee has the right to refuse participating in discussion without union representation. While a union representative may not directly advise the employee, he/she may ask questions or provide information that may affect the employer's decision.

Source: http://en.wikipedia.org/wiki/Weingarten_Rights

Global Employee Relations

Many organizations operate in a global environment where employment issues, employment laws, and business practices can vary dramatically from country to country. HR professionals working in multinational companies must have a global perspective a solid grasp of international employment issues to help the organization run smoothly. For multinational employers, there are unique employee relations issues to manage. Employees abroad may have unique health and safety issues due to political conditions, regulations, economic conditions, or physical environment. Additionally, the employer must also comply with the laws of the countries in which it operates[55].

Global Health and Safety

Addressing safety and health issues are an important role for HR practitioners. Employees working abroad may not have the same level of healthcare access or as safe of an environment as the U.S. location. HR practitioners can work to develop policies and employment benefits that support the employees. Companies may offer private insurance plans or funds for medical assistance to protect the health of employees. These policies, however, must comply with the country's laws and should be a generally accepted business practice in that country.

Depending on the regions in which they operate, international organizations may also have to deal with the threat of terrorism. Certain people, such as U.S. citizens or those who appear wealthy, may also be vulnerable to kidnapping, harassment, extortion, and other violence in regions that are experiencing anti-U.S. sentiment or political unrest. These dangers can occur either on or near the worksite, or near the employees' homes. To protect employees in working in dangerous areas, many firms provide bodyguards to escort executives wherever they go; different routes of travel to make it difficult for criminals to track an individual; and safety training for family members of employees. Some companies may secure the grounds of their facilities with fences, barricades, armed guards, metal detectors, and/or surveillance devices. Others may take steps to minimize the visibility of the company, if there is hostility toward the U.S. in that area.

To ensure the safety of expatriates (i.e. American citizens working abroad), the company may provide emergency protective services through International SOS or another reputable organization that can refer the ill or injured employee to adequate medical care if available locally, dispatch physicians, or transport employees to safety via aircraft. Additional safeguards

---

[55] Source: http://www.shrm.org/hrdisciplines/employeerelations/Pages/GlobalEmployeeRelations.aspx

may include legal counsel that practices in the country, or emergency cash for medical expenses or travel home.

Cultural Differences and Work Ethic

Cultural norms in a country or region influence how people act and interact with one another. When employing international workers, the organization should be clear about its expectations of all its workers, regardless of geography. At the same time, in order to sustain successful operations in a country, an employer should understand the norms, values, and attitudes of the workers there. If the organization's values are completely contrary to the culture of a region or country, it can lead to extreme conflict if not managed properly. Having flexibility for certain cultural practices while taking meaningful action to assimilate employees into the organization can make the situation more successful. For example, if a US-based company has operations in the Middle East, it will need to allow (and enforce) more traditional forms of attire that are customary in that region. Cultural differences among international employees can lead to different attitudes toward work and therefore different work ethic. It is important for HR practitioners and management to recognize these differences and gain an understanding of how these may affect their interaction with the rest of the company. HR practitioners can play a key role in facilitating open dialogue and providing learning opportunities for both U.S. and non-U.S. employees to work together more effectively.

Global Labor Relations

The impact and nature of labor unions varies from country to country. In some places, such as China or African countries, unions do not exist or are relatively weak. In other places, such as Europe, unions are extremely strong and may be closely aligned with political parties. In other places, such as the United States, unions have declined in influence and membership over time. These differences affect how collective bargaining occurs, too. In the United States, independent unions bargain with the employer on working conditions and wages. In Europe, however, bargaining is typically done industry-wide or regionally. Some countries require that companies have union representatives on their boards of directors (called co-determination)[56]. It is important for multinational organizations to understand the norms of a country and be prepared to work with organized labor where it is present, in the manner that is customary for that country or region.

---

[56] Source: http://www.bls.gov/opub/mlr/2006/01/art3full.pdf

Review

Main Ideas to Remember

→ Employee relations is the maintenance of employer-employee relationships to maintain high productivity and morale. When conducted effectively, it improves the understanding of the organization's policies, procedures, and expectations to employees. People who handle employee relations deal with conflict, poor behavior, and difficult situations – and identify ways to both prevent and resolve those types of issues through special programs and communications.

→ An employee's manager or department may have his or her own specific procedures and expectations that are typically aligned with those of the overall organization. When employees are not performing well or behave in an unacceptable manner, the manager will counsel the employee, identify the issues, and discuss a plan to correct the problem.

→ When an employee files a complaint about his or her work conditions, management or HR will discuss the concerns, investigate if necessary, and collect key data to make an informed decision. In serious situations such as sexual harassment or discrimination, employees are typically reminded of their grievance and appeal rights and discrimination, as well as any whistleblower protections.

→ *Organizational culture* is the workplace environment that is fostered by both leadership and employees. At its very essence, it describes how people within the organization interact with one another, and it is affected by the experiences, personalities, values, beliefs, and principles of leadership and employees. An organization's culture affects its overall identity and the way that employees, clients, and the general public view the organization.

→ The U.S. Department of Labor (DOL) administers and enforces more than 180 federal laws. These mandates and the regulations that implement them cover many workplace activities for many organizations that employee people.

→ The Fair Labor Standards Act (FLSA) mandates standards for the payment of regular wages and overtime, which affect most private and public employers.

→ The Occupational Safety and Health Act regulates the safety and health of employees, and is administered by the Occupational Safety and Health Administration (OSHA), who may conduct inspections and investigations.

→ Under USERRA, certain employees who serve in the armed forces have a right to reemployment with the employer they were with when they entered service, including reserves and National Guard.

→ The Employee Polygraph Protection Act prohibits most employers from using lie detectors on employees, but permits polygraph tests only in limited circumstances.

→ Many labor-related, public safety and environmental laws protect whistleblowers—in general, employees who make good faith complaints about violations of the law committed by their employers. Penalties for violating these protections can include job reinstatement and payment of back wages.

→ Recipients of government contracts, grants or financial aid are subject to their own set of wage, hour, benefits, and safety and health standards under the following laws: Davis-Bacon Act; McNamara-O'Hara Service Contract Act; and Walsh-Healy Public Contracts Act. Government contractors are also required to comply with federal affirmative action and equal opportunity laws, executive orders, and regulations.

→ Individual states (and sometimes localities) create and enforce their own laws related to the employment of workers. Employers should be aware of the employment laws in all states in which they conduct business and have employees; the state's Department of Labor can be contacted for information about employment laws in that particular state.

→ An employee handbook, also referred to as an employee manual, is a document of the organization's policies and procedures that affect all employees. It can provide both employment and practical information such as company rules, performance expectations, and office operations. A written employee handbook gives clear guidance to employees, sets expectations and creates a culture where issues are dealt with fairly and consistently.

→ An *"employment-at-will" statement* specifies that an employee or employer may terminate the employment relationship, with or without reason, and with or without notice. In an at-will employment situation (which is the case in many states), there is no expectation of employment either indefinitely or for a specified duration

→ Handbooks can be a useful tool in situations when corrective action needs to be taken on an employee, up to and including termination of employment. When writing up employees or terminating them, it is helpful to refer to the specific policy or policies that are being violated.

→ *Labor relations* describes the interaction between employers and employees, typically in a unionized environment. (However, in some cases it applies to non-union workers as well.) When labor relations are strong at an organization, management works effectively with employee representatives (typically labor unions) to solve problems in ways that are both in the interest of the employee and the organization.

→ The National Labor Relations Act of 1935 (also called the Wagner Act) granted most *private-sector* workers a large number of labor rights, including the right to strike, to bargain as a union, and to protest the conditions of their employment.

→ Employees covered by the Wagner Act are granted certain rights to join together to improve their wages and working conditions, with or without a union. This means that although a union may not be present in an organization, employees at that organization still have rights to talk about the conditions of their employment with one another and take action as a group, as discussed below.

→ Concerted activity occurs when two or more employees take action for their mutual benefit or protection with respect to the conditions or terms of their employment. It is protected by the NLRA.

→ The effects of the NLRA were changed substantially when the Taft-Hartley Act was passed in 1947. Taft-Hartley outlawed closed shops, jurisdictional strikes, and secondary boycotts. It set up mechanisms for decertifying unions and allowed states to pass certain anti-union legislation such as right-to-work laws.

→ Employee complaints can range in scope, but generally are not severe. They can alert management of a problem before it grows out of control, and give management a chance to respond and show its commitment to addressing employee concerns.

→ Grievances are formal complaints made by employees when they believe a company policy, a collective bargaining agreement, or a law, has been violated. Grievances are red flags warning HR and management about large problems that require immediate attention. A prompt response that results in quick resolution will improve employee morale and productivity and can potentially prevent costly legal action.

→ Taking steps of progressive discipline is typically useful for non-serious offenses that are repetitive, or where there is no indication of improvement by the employee. These steps include verbal warning, written warning, probation, suspension, and termination. Some employers, especially those subject to collective bargaining agreements, require a strict use of each step in succession. Others, however, reserve the right to use any or all steps necessary to address a particular issue.

→ For multinational employers, there are unique employee relations issues to manage. Employees abroad may have unique health and safety issues due to political conditions, regulations, economic conditions, or physical environment. The employer must also comply with the laws of the countries in which it operates.

Key Terms to Review

Agency shop

Arbitration

Bargaining unit

Closed shop

COBRA

Collective bargaining

Complaint

Concerted activity

Consumer Credit Protection Act

Davis-Bacon Act

Employee handbook

Employee Polygraph Protection Act

Employee relations

Employment at will

ERISA

Executive Order 10988

Fair Labor Standards Act

Family and Medical Leave Act (FMLA)

Grievance

HIPAA

Labor relations

Labor union

Lockout

McNamara-O'Hara Service Contract Act

National Labor Relations Act of 1935

Occupational Safety and Health Act

OFCCP

Open shop

Organizational culture

Patient Protection and Affordable Care Act

Performance improvement plan

Picketing

Probation

Progressive discipline

Right-to-work law

Seniority

Suspension

Taft-Hartley Act

Termination of employment

Unfair labor practice

Union security clause

Union shop

USERRA

Verbal warning

Wagner Act

Walsh-Healy Public Contracts Act

WARN Act

Weingarten rights

Whistleblower

Written warning

Risk Management

Section Overview

→ What is compliance, and why is it important to organizations?

→ What types of rules do organizations need to follow?

→ What are regulations, and how are they similar to laws? Why are they important to organizations?

→ What responsibilities does an organization have to the health and welfare of employees?

→ What kinds of hazards can be found in a workplace? How do organizations deal with hazards?

→ How can organizations keep their resources safe?

→ What role does HR have in keeping employees safe?

→ What is business continuity, and how do organizations plan for it?

→ What role does HR have in business continuity and recovery plans?

→ What privacy concerns do employers face?

→ What laws govern the protection of employee information and privacy?

→ How do employees handle workplace monitoring and searches?

Legal Compliance

Compliance means different things depending on the company or industry. However, at minimum, all companies with employees must comply with federal and state employment laws. Many of these laws, such as the Fair Labor Standards Act and Occupational Safety and Health Act, have been described throughout this guide. It is the responsibility of employers to understand all the laws that apply to their business in the locations in which they operate. These companies should develop sound policies that are well documented, and train employees to ensure they can understand and follow them. There should also be procedures for handling employees who do not comply with a company policy (and may therefore be non-compliant with the law).

Not only do companies have to be compliant with laws, they also have to understand and follow regulations, which are specific directives with the same force of law enacted by federal agencies to execute acts passed by Congress. The Family and Medical Leave Act is an example of a law passed by Congress that resulted in regulations and procedures developed by the Department of Labor, the regulatory agency that implements the law. The Internal Revenue Service (IRS) also creates regulations that can affect employee payroll and benefits.

The Federal Rulemaking Process

The Administration Procedure Act outlines the method in which federal rules must be proposed, amended, and finalized. The following are the basic steps for promulgating a federal rule or regulation:

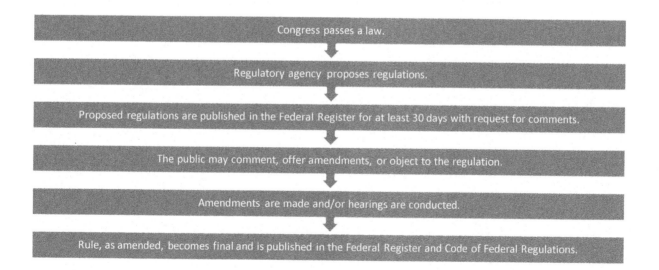

The applicable law (which the regulation supports) specifies the process used to create accompanying regulations. Some regulations require only publication and an opportunity for comments to become final. Others require publication and formal public hearings. Once a regulation becomes "final rule" and takes effect, it is published in the Federal Register, the Code of Federal Regulations (CFR), and on the website of the regulatory agency.

Safety and Health

Organizations have a responsibility to protect the safety, health and well-being of their employees. Safety and health is a moral obligation because it involves the lives and health of employees, and ensuring their safety is the right thing to do. At the same time, there are also legal obligations that an employer has to ensure employee safety and health; such laws have specific guidelines employers must follow and certain penalties and fines for employers that do not follow the law. Taking the necessary precautions can also reduce costs the business may incur, including the costs of medical care, sick leave, disability benefits, and lost productivity.

Depending on the nature of the business and where it conducts its operations, there are a number of health and safety hazards and risks that employees may face. A **workplace hazard** is something that can cause harm if it is not mitigated or eliminated. **Risk** is defined as the probability that a specific outcome (i.e. harm) will occur. It is the role of HR professionals or safety professionals to identify hazards and assess risks that affect employers, for the moral, legal, and financial reasons described above.

In general, there are three categories of workplace hazards that are described below: physical, chemical, and psychosocial. Certain industries may have a greater likelihood of certain hazards over others. For example, the construction industry may have more physical than chemical hazards, while the financial industry may have numerous psychosocial hazards but very limited physical hazards.

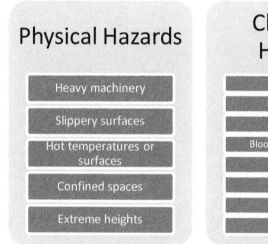
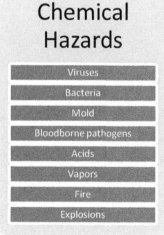

HR and safety officers can take a series of measures to mitigate workplace hazards. They should develop methods and procedures to manage hazards that can cause injury to their workers and their facilities. Workspaces, equipment, procedures, and services should periodically be evaluated for safety, and employees should be actively included in developing safe working practices. Resources should be allocated to train employees on safety and enforce safety rules. Safety rules and procedures should be evaluated for their effectiveness periodically, with the input of management and employees.

To be effective, people who manage safety at an organization need to have a certain body of knowledge. They need to be well versed in laws and regulations that govern employee health and safety (such as the Organizational Safety and Health Act) as well as industry standards on best practices. They need to be able to design operational procedures as well as recordkeeping systems for clarity and accountability. They should also be able to identify and implement safety equipment and resources necessary to protect employees as they conduct their jobs.

Security

Just as a home needs to be secure from intruders, an organization also has security needs. A data breach, for example, can lead to key information being leaked to competitors and harm the organization financially. An intruder breaking in to the company's headquarters can steal important records that can also lead to a number of losses and headaches for the organization. Protecting the security of the organization's employees (physically), facilities, infrastructure, and resources is vital to its survival. An organization should carefully plan its security strategy.

Chart: Components of Organizational Security

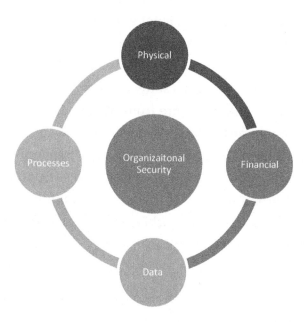

1. Develop security policies and procedures that are well documented and published for all employees to access. Having this documentation makes the organization's commitment to security clear, and takes out much of the "guesswork" with management, who enforces security concerns on a day-to-day basis.

2. Maintain a physically secure environment. If the business is at risk of theft, robberies, violence, or other crimes, it is important to install surveillance, secure entries, metal detectors, and other devices that are necessary to monitor the premises and prevent mishaps. The organization should also have policies and procedures that relate to employees' handling of company equipment including computers. The policies should clearly indicate what steps the employee should take when company property is lost or stolen, so that the organization can respond appropriately and mitigate the effects of that loss.

3. Restrict information to those who only need to know. Employees should only have access to files, records, and information that are necessary to conduct their jobs. Limit access to sensitive information only to those who need it in order to perform a certain function or are in a position to make decisions related to that information. Additionally,

the company should have a policy in place that requires employees to maintain confidentiality of any sensitive or proprietary information they have access to.

4. Protect data from loss, theft, or intrusion. A number of viruses and malware running rampant on the internet, as well as the risk of cyber-attacks, can wreak havoc on the organization's technological infrastructure. The organization should take precautions by installing the appropriate firewalls, anti-virus software, and network monitoring software necessary to protect its infrastructure from attacks. Employees should be required to maintain a computer and network password that is hard to guess, and require that passwords be changed on a periodic basis. The organization should have "acceptable use" policies which restrict employees from accessing non-work related websites (to minimize inadvertent downloads that can be harmful to their computer or even the entire network); this can usually be achieved by installing web filtering software on the network.

5. Protect financial assets from loss or theft. If the company deals with the general public, and employees have access to certain cash reserves, protocols should be in place to monitor the flow of money and require employees to balance cash at the end of their shifts. The company should also protect any reserves it has on-site by using a state-of-the-art safe, and it should limit the funds it keeps on premises to an amount that is necessary to conduct daily business.

6. Train employees on security practices and hold them accountable. Poor training often leads to security breaches, and thorough training conducted periodically will keep employees aware and invested in the security of the business.

Business Continuity

In this day and age, disasters such as destructive hurricanes, fires, or terrorist attacks, can strike at any time, and organizations should take careful steps to be prepared. HR practitioners are a valuable partner in business continuity planning through the development of policies and procedures, as well as managing all the "people" aspects of business continuity, including staffing plans, medical emergencies, allocation of resources, and employee concerns. The planning and execution of business continuity processes fall in four phases, as outlined below[57].

Chart: The phases of business continuity

Planning Phase

During the planning phase, HR practitioners help the organization to develop clear goals, procedures, and expectations that are communicated to employees. Typically, these policies are included in the employee handbook, and employees are trained and re-trained on a periodic basis. The policies and procedures should outline important information the employees need to know, for example:

- How the business plans to continue operations in the event of disaster

- The employee's role in keeping in touch with the employer

- How employees should handle certain hazards such as fire or power outages

---

[57] Source: http://www.drj.com/drworld/content/w3_021.htm

- How the organization will notify employees of changes to business operations or safety procedures during a disaster.

Additionally, the business should develop a more detailed business continuity plan that outlines important details about how the business will recover assets, mobilize employees, continue operations, and compensate employees. The recovery plan should address all the logistics necessary to mitigate losses to the business, such as:

- Who is responsible for notifying authorities? How will first responders obtain access to the facilities?

- How will employees be evacuated? What will the company do to help employees find medical attention and safety if necessary?

- Where will employees work? Where will they stay? How will the company keep track of where employees are?

- How will employees be paid?

- What resources do they need to continue doing their jobs, and how will the company provide these resources?

- How will the company's data, files, and information be protected to prevent disaster and recover from disaster? Are backup copies maintained remotely?

It is best to pre-plan for all issues before disaster occurs, while planners have an opportunity to think clearly and thoroughly. HR professionals can play a key role in ensuring that the organization is ready to handle disasters and prepare to help manage employees' whereabouts, safety, and business operations. Having detailed procedures that outline "who does what" at each step will help keep the flow of communication open and help the process move efficiently. Employees should clearly understand their roles for the recovery process and should be trained periodically.

Recovery

During the recovery period, after disaster strikes, the organization will need to adapt to operating differently for a period of time. For example, employees may need to work remotely; certain services or production of products may be put on hold; or the hours of operation may be different than normal. The organization's HR department can play a critical role during this phase by working side by side with managers to deploy and track staff and resources to keep the business running. HR can notify employees of their roles, hours, and expectations of work during the recovery period. They can fill in staffing gaps by hiring temporary staff. They can also respond to employees' immediate concerns and notify management of issues that need to be handled. HR can help fulfill employees' immediate needs by deploying emergency food, shelter, cash, or goods if the employee is required to be away from home and the normal worksite. Additionally, if employees are ill or injured, HR can notify family members and keep them informed. Having these needs met will help able-bodied employees to keep the business running as smoothly as possible despite changes in conditions.

Post-Recovery

Once the recovery period has ended and the company is ready to resume operations, HR's role is to notify employees and help transition them back to normal operations. If the surrounding area has been severely damaged, HR will need to respond to employees' needs for time off to find a new home, recover from injuries, or take care of personal and family matters. During this period, it is important for the organization to remain as flexible as possible with employees and recognizing their efforts to continue balancing their personal and work responsibilities. Recognizing employees for their resilience and dedication to helping the organization succeed will help keep morale higher. If employees feel that their needs are respected and that they are appreciated by the organization, they are more likely to remain loyal to the organization.

HR plays an important role during the planning and execution of business continuity procedures. If these processes are overlooked, it can be detrimental to the long-term success of the business and the well-being of employees. Involving HR, management, and employees in each step of the process and keeping communication open and clear will help position the organization to weather disaster and protect its employees and assets.

Privacy and Confidentiality

Managing the organization's safety and security can lead to privacy concerns. On one hand, the organization needs to carefully monitor and protect its assets, while employees have a desire for a certain degree of privacy in their day-to-day activities. To manage risk, organizations may take a number of measures, such as monitoring computer usage, conducting background checks of employees, and tracking people who enter and exit facilities. In general, employees in the U.S. should have no broad expectation of privacy, and the employer has a right to monitor and protect its assets; however, there are federal and state laws that protect the privacy of employees to some degree. When implementing certain measures, it is important for the organization to understand whether the activity is lawful and weigh how effectively each practice achieves a specific business need.

Protected Information

As a rule, only personally identifiable information, such as a person's name or Social Security Number, is afforded special protection by data privacy laws. In some cases, a combination of information such as birth date, address, and gender, can be used to identify an individual and is therefore considered protected information. There are federal and state laws that govern the usage and sharing of personally identifiable information:

- *Health Insurance Portability and Accountability Act* (HIPAA) – protects health-related information with covered entities such as insurance plans.

- *Genetic Information Nondiscrimination Act* (GINA) – protects and restricts the usage of employees' genetic information.

- *Fair Credit Reporting Act* (FCRA) – restricts the ways that consumer data, such as credit reports, may be used for employment purposes

Many U.S. states have their own laws concerning data security and notifications of breaches, and organizations should be aware of all data security laws in the states in which they operate. Additionally, companies have a responsibility under the law not only to protect employee information, but also that of job applicants, independent contractors, and customers. Companies that operate internationally should also be aware of the laws in each country in which they operate and implement the most stringent security mechanisms that comply with all laws with which they need to comply. Even if there is no law that specifically requires the protection of certain data, it is still a best practice for the organization to ensure that all personal information, whether protected or not protected by law, is safe from breaches. Keeping documents of active employees secure and discarding data that is no longer needed (as allowed by recordkeeping laws and regulations) can help manage the organization's risk. Employers can also protect data by disclosing it only to parties on a need to know basis, with the explicit authorization of the employee, or by virtue of a court order. Data should be provided using the most secure means as possible, such as encrypted email or facsimile, and there should be specific procedures in place if a data breach occurs. Because HR professionals often work with personal data on a regular basis, it is important that they maintain confidentiality to the greatest extent possible and take careful measures not to compromise the security of data.

Workplace Monitoring and Searches

It is common for employees to monitor the computer, email, web, and phone usage of employees for quality control and security. They may also implement drug and alcohol testing to ensure the safety of employees and prevent accidents or injuries.

As a best practice, and to comply with various privacy laws, the organization should notify employees (i.e. typically in a handbook) that they should have no expectation of privacy when on the premises or when using company resources, and the specific ways in which the company may monitor employees. Companies should contact a qualified attorney to understand their limits for employee surveillance, drug testing, and personal searches by virtue of federal and state law. For example, companies may not put cameras in restrooms, but they may have cameras monitoring a cash register[58]. Employers may also be limited by how they can conduct personal searches and may not force employees to submit to a search; however, they may rightfully terminate employees who refuse.

Having clear policies that are applied consistently to all employees will help the organization set expectations and manage risk. If employees understand what is expected of them as well as the consequences for noncompliance, and if they understand that the rules are enforced universally, the organization can help protect itself against claims of unfair treatment or discrimination while promoting a safe workplace.

---

[58] Source: http://smallbusiness.chron.com/employee-privacy-rights-1239.html

Review

Main Ideas to Remember

→ All companies with employees must comply with federal and state employment laws. It is the responsibility of employers to understand all the laws that apply to their business in the locations in which they operate. These companies should develop sound policies that are well documented, and train employees to ensure they can understand and follow them.

→ Not only do companies have to be compliant with laws; they also have to understand and follow regulations, which are specific directives with the same force of law, that are enacted by federal agencies to execute acts passed by Congress.

→ Organizations have a responsibility to protect the safety, health and well-being of their employees. Safety and health is a moral obligation because it involves the lives and health of employees, and ensuring their safety is the right thing to do. At the same time, there are also legal obligations that an employer has to ensure employee safety and health; such laws have specific guidelines employers must follow and certain penalties and fines for employers that do not follow the law.

→ A workplace hazard is something that can cause harm if it is not mitigated or eliminated. Risk is defined as the probability that a specific outcome (i.e. harm) will occur. It is the role of HR professionals or safety professionals to identify hazards and assess risks that affect employers.

→ There are three categories of workplace hazards: physical, chemical, and psychosocial. Certain industries may have a greater likelihood of certain hazards.

→ HR and safety officers can take a series of measures to mitigate workplace hazards. They should develop methods and procedures to manage hazards that can cause injury to their workers and their facilities. Workspaces, equipment, procedures, and services should periodically be evaluated for safety, and employees should be actively included in developing safe working practices. Resources should be allocated to train employees on safety and enforce safety rules. Safety rules and procedures should be evaluated for their effectiveness periodically, with the input of management and employees.

→ Protecting the security of the organization's employees (physically), facilities, infrastructure, and resources is vital to its survival. An organization should carefully plan its security strategy, which includes developing security policies, restricting information, protecting data and infrastructure, and maintaining a physically secure environment.

→ HR practitioners are a valuable partner in business continuity planning through the development of policies and procedures, as well as managing all the "people" aspects of business continuity, including staffing plans, medical emergencies, allocation of resources, and employee concerns.

→ The phases of business continuity are planning, emergency response, recovery, and post-recovery. Involving HR, management, and employees in each step of the process, and keeping communication open and clear, will help position the organization to weather disaster and protect its employees and assets.

→ To manage risk, organizations may take a number of measures, such as monitoring computer usage, conducting background checks of employees, and tracking people who enter and exit facilities. These activities, however, can lead to privacy concerns. Companies should weigh the effectiveness of these measures as well as understand the legalities surrounding them

Key Terms to Review

Business continuity

Confidentiality

FCRA

Federal rulemaking process

GINA

Hazard

HIPAA

Post-recovery

Privacy

Recovery

Regulations

Regulatory compliance

Risk

Security

Types of hazards

Workplace monitoring

Workplace searches

.

Practice Examination

1. An employer has the right to:

    a. Forbid employees from discussing union membership or activities

    b. Terminate two non-union employees for discussing the conditions of their job

    c. Describe a union's strike history and the economic consequences of strikes

    d. Give preferential treatment to one union over another

2. Leadership theories that look at the personal characteristics of a leader are:

    a. Trait theories

    b. Situational theories

    c. Behavioral theories

    d. Contingency theories

3. To be effective, company goals must:

    a. Require the participation of line staff

    b. Be available in multiple languages

    c. Grow the company

    d. Be specific and measurable

4. The party responsible for verifying that an employee is eligible to work in the United States is:

    a. USCIS

    b. Department of Labor

    c. Employer

    d. Employee

5. What is employee training?

    a. The development of skills that apply to an employee's job

    b. Teaching employees about their requirements

    c. One-on-one tutoring

    d. An intervention of employees who need special attention

6. Which of the following HR responsibilities is most likely to differ from country to country?

    a. Job analysis

    b. Training and development

    c. Compensation and benefits

    d. Personnel records

7. The "prudent person rule" is associated with which law?

    a. FLSA

    b. ERISA

    c. FMLA

    d. OSHA

8. Which is generally true about executive compensation?

    a. Executives receive a wider variety of compensation than other employees

    b. Executives receive cheaper health insurance than other employees

    c. Executives are guaranteed pay even if they do not work

    d. Executives do not receive a base salary

9. Which of the following strategies is associated with workforce expansion?

    a. outsourcing

    b. demotions

    c. management training

    d. job rotations

10. The Civil Rights Act of 1964 does not prohibit discrimination on which of the following?

    a. Color

    b. Religion

    c. Race

    d. Age

11. Which of the following career development strategies best promotes a wide range of skills?

    a. Job rotation

    b. Job shadowing

    c. Job sharing

    d. Flexible work arrangements

12. Workers' Compensation provides benefits for:

    a. Dependents in the event of the employee's death

    b. Pregnancy

    c. Job-related injuries or death

    d. Retirement

13. Which of the following benefits is/are not required by law?

    a. Life insurance

    b. Health insurance

    c. Retirement plan

    d. All of the above

14. The primary purpose of an HR audit is to:

    a. Provide information to the federal government

    b. Determine how many HR staff are needed

    c. Evaluate the effectiveness of the HR function

    d. Determine which HRIS system to use

15. A written description of the work performed by an employee is called a/an:

    a. Job specification

    b. Job description

    c. At-will employment statement

    d. Compensation analysis

16. Which of the following statements about Affirmative Action Plans is true?

    a. All employers with over 100 employees are required to have an AAP.

    b. An AAP is required for employers who have been found to discriminate against employees.

    c. An AAP is required by the Fair Labor Standards Act.

    d. An AAP must be signed by a company officer and made available to internal employees and vendors

17. The least serious OSHA violation is:

    a. Serious

    b. Other-than-serious

    c. De minimus

    d. Non-qualified

18. Which federal agency has the primary responsibility to enforce employment non-discrimination laws?

    a. Department of Labor

    b. Equal Employment Opportunity Commission

    c. National Association for the Advancement of Colored People

    d. Office of the Attorney General

19. COBRA allows a terminated employee to continue coverage under the employer's health insurance policy for how long?

    a. 12 months

    b. 18 months

    c. 36 months

    d. Indefinitely

20. Which types of employees cannot be represented by a union under the NLRA?

    a. Supervisors, confidential employees, and managers

    b. Seasonal employees, managers, and supervisors

    c. Supervisors and key employees

    d. Managers, supervisors, and non-US citizens

21. The two primary dimensions of behavioral theories of leadership are:

   a. Common sense and task-relevant knowledge

   b. Consideration and initiating structure

   c. Self-confidence and initiating structure

   d. Initiating structure and task-relevant knowledge

22. Which of the following laws allows employers to establish drug testing policies?

   a. Occupational Safety and Health Act

   b. Drug Free Workplace Act

   c. Equal Employment Opportunity

   d. Drug Testing Act

23. A consistent wage despite the number of hours worked is called:

   a. Salary

   b. Bonus

   c. Variable pay

   d. Base pay

24. Which of the following factors is considered in an environmental scan?

   a. Competition

   b. Succession plan

   c. Staffing metrics

   d. Compensation analysis

25. **Which of the following laws deals directly with pay discrimination?**

    a. Fair Labor Standards Act

    b. Affirmative Action

    c. PPACA

    d. Equal Pay Act

26. **The centralized approach to compensation works best when:**

    a. The company wants to pay the same wages to US and non-US employees.

    b. The other countries have a low standard of living

    c. There are few international employees

    d. Inflation is low

27. **Which of the following is typically considered a taxable benefit?**

    a. Vacation pay

    b. Health insurance

    c. Flexible spending account

    d. 401(k) matching contribution

28. **Which of the following recruitment methods is likely to result in greater loyalty?**

    a. Campus recruiting

    b. Internet job board

    c. Employee referrals

    d. Newspaper ad

29. The Fair Credit Reporting Act requires an employer to:

a. Obtain written authorization from an applicant before conducting a credit check

b. Use credit checks to verify an applicant's eligibility to work

c. Conduct a credit check secretly

d. Provide verbal notification that a credit check will be completed on a prospective employee

30. Disparate treatment occurs when:

a. A neutral compensation practice results in unintentional wage discrimination

b. Affirmative Action Plans are put into place

c. An employee who is a member of a protected class is intentionally paid less

d. Employees are all eligible for pay-for-performance compensation

31. What is the main purpose of a grievance procedure?

a. To resolve conflict

b. To empower employees to go on strike

c. To terminate employees

d. To provide progressive discipline

32. "Reasonable accommodation" is a term associated with which federal statute?

a. Americans with Disabilities Act

b. Civil Rights Act of 1964

c. Wagner Act

d. Fair Labor Standards Act

33. Which type of learning curve gradually increases in pace with larger increments?

    a. S-shaped learning curve

    b. Positively accelerating learning curve

    c. Negatively accelerating learning curve

    d. Plateau

34. What is the last and final step of a grievance procedure?

    a. NLRB ruling

    b. Third-party arbitration

    c. Union representative and management

    d. Strike

35. The Family and Medical Leave Act requires employers to:

    a. Provide affordable health insurance to employees and their dependents.

    b. Provide employees with up to 12 weeks of paid leave for surgeries and sickness.

    c. Provide Workers' Comp insurance to employees who are injured on the job

    d. Give employees up to 12 weeks of unpaid leave to care for themselves or a family member with a serious health condition

36. What is the core of labor relations?

    a. Collective bargaining

    b. Union dues

    c. Right-to-work laws

    d. Strikes and lock-outs

37. Employment at will means:

    a. The employee is guaranteed a job only for a specified amount of time

    b. The employee or employer may terminate the relationship at any time

    c. Employees may only be fired for serious offenses

    d. Employees must have an employment contract with the employer

38. Which agency is responsible for enforcing federal laws regarding safety on the job?

    a. Bureau of Labor Statistics

    b. Department of Commerce

    c. Occupational Safety and Health Administration

    d. USCIS

39. Which is not a category of exempt status under the Fair Labor Standards Act?

    a. Outside sales

    b. Management

    c. Salaried Assistants

    d. Executives

40. Which is <u>not</u> one of the criteria for evaluating training programs?

    a. Synthesis

    b. Reactions

    c. Learning

    d. Behavior

41. Which of the following federal laws applies to most employers?

    a. Rehabilitation Act of 1973

    b. Vietnam-Era Veterans Readjustment Act

    c. Age Discrimination in Employment Act

    d. Affirmative Action

42. A company wsants to restructure a department. What role would HR likely <u>not</u> play?

    a. Develop a project plan for handling the restructuring

    b. Design new products and services

    c. Write job descriptions for the new or refined positions

    d. Assess the skills and competencies of staff

43. An organization has many detailed procedures and is resistant to change. Which phase of the organizational life cycle does this describe?

    a. Birth

    b. Growth

    c. Maturity

    d. Decline

44. How long must employers keep records of occupational illnesses, injuries, and incidents?

    a. 1 year

    b. 5 years

    c. 10 years

    d. Indefinitely

45. What is the purpose of an Employee Assistance Program?

    a. Provide free, confidential counseling on work/life and personal matters

    b. Assist employees with finding a job when they are laid off

    c. Help employers find the best candidates for a position

    d. Provide legal counsel to employees who want to sue the company

46. The primary reason employee handbooks should be reviewed carefully and continually updated is because they may:

    a. Be available to the public for review

    b. Create an enforceable contract

    c. Provide new employees with important information

    d. Be the only way the employer communicates with employees

47. Decentralization works best in organizations where:

    a. Employees dislike management

    b. Unions are present

    c. The organization is too top-heavy

    d. A quick response to problems is needed

48. An employee removes his safety glasses because they are uncomfortable. He gets a chemical in his eye and requires medical treatment. This is an example of an:

    a. Unsafe act

    b. Unfair treatment

    c. Organizational risk

    d. Unsafe work environment

49. ERISA was designed to protect employee rights in what area?

    a. Retirement plans

    b. Unemployment compensation

    c. Workers' Compensation

    d. Recruitment and hiring

50. Which are terms associated with selecting a market position for base salaries?

    a. Lead

    b. Match

    c. Lag

    d. All the above

51. A practitioner with expertise in a limited area of human resources is called:

    a. HR generalist

    b. HR manager

    c. HR specialist

    d. None of the above

52. Who does <u>not</u> typically appraise an employee's performance in a 360-degree performance appraisal system?

    a. Peers

    b. Subordinates

    c. Current supervisor

    d. None of the above

53. Behavioral-based training includes all of the following except:

    a. Diversity training

    b. Internship

    c. Case studies/incidents

    d. Business games

54. What is the main reason employers offer a comprehensive benefits package?

    a. To reduce operating costs

    b. To do what other companies are doing

    c. To help attract and retain employees

    d. To save money on taxes

55. Which form of compensation is typically reserved for executives?

    a. Base pay

    b. Bonus

    c. Stock options

    d. Differential pay

56. The FMLA requires employers having ___ employees within a 50-mile radius to provide job-protected leave to qualified employees for medical reasons.

    a. 10

    b. 25

    c. 50

    d. 100

57. Which law governs the number of hours that children may work?

    a. FLSA

    b. ADEA

    c. FMLA

    d. IRCA

58. If a non-exempt employee is off for Memorial Day but works 10 hours a day the rest of the week, how many hours of overtime pay is she entitled to under the FLSA?

    a. 0

    b. 8

    c. 40

    d. 48

59. Which of the following is not a type of retirement plan?

    a. Defined contribution plan

    b. Defined benefit plan

    c. Defined retirement age plan

    d. Profit sharing plan

60. Which is an example(s) of pay for performance?

    a. Variable pay

    b. Piecework

    c. Gainsharing

    d. All of the above

61. Health insurance benefits are a component of:

    a. Total rewards

    b. Organizational development

    c. Work-life balance

    d. Pay for performance

62. Title VII allows an employer to discriminate on the basis of sex, religion, or national origin if these are a "bona fide occupational qualification." Which jobs might apply?

    a. Teacher

    b. Doctor

    c. Fashion model

    d. Police officer

63. The OSHA Form 300 must be completed:

    a. When an employee dies due to a work-related illness or injury

    b. When a work-related injury leads to missed days

    c. When a work-related injury requires medical care beyond first aid

    d. All of the above

64. How much notice must a company give the bargaining unit if it wants to change the terms of a collective bargaining agreement while it is in effect?

    a. 30 days

    b. 60 days

    c. 90 days

    d. 120 days

65. Which of the following activities is typical of the transactional leader?

    a. Allows workers to be autonomous

    b. Gets involved when standards are not met

    c. Micromanages employees

    d. Sets unrealistic expectations

66. An applicant applying for which of the following positions may be required to take a polygraph test?

    a. A teacher working with small kids

    b. A cashier at a grocery store

    c. An agent at an insurance company

    d. A delivery driver for a pharmaceutical company

67. A closed shop is a company that:

    a. Refuses to hire union members

    b. Requires employees to become union members

    c. Sponsors a union

    d. Applies to all unionized workplaces

68. What theory includes the elements of safety/security needs and self-actualization?

    a. Maslow's hierarchy

    b. Myers Briggs

    c. Leadership theory

    d. Equality theory

69. Which is a method of comparing the relative performance of employees?

    a. Structuring

    b. Pay for performance

    c. Ranking

    d. Performance improvement plan

70. Which document confirms an employee's identity and verifies his/her right to work in the U.S., for purposes of the I-9 form?

    a. Unexpired U.S. passport

    b. Driver's license

    c. Birth certificate

    d. Foreign passport

71. The four distinct stages for HR planning do not include:

    a. Action plans

    b. HR systems analysis

    c. Environmental scanning

    d. Forecasting

72. What is the difference between Affirmative Action and Equal Employment Opportunity?

    a. Equal Employment Opportunity is required by law

    b. Affirmative action promotes fair employment classes

    c. Affirmative Action is required of government contractors

    d. Equal Employment Opportunity sets quotas for hiring.

73. Which of the following elements is part of a company's "compensation philosophy"?

    a. Fixed and variable pay

    b. Pay in relation to the market

    c. Pay for the job

    d. All of the above

74. Strategic HR management includes the following activity:

    a. Planning

    b. Developing objectives

    c. Aligning resources

    d. All of the above

75. Which would be considered a bona fide occupational requirement for firefighters?

    a. Applicants must be at least 5'5"

    b. Applicants must be able to handle extreme temperatures

    c. Applicants must be a U.S. Citizen

    d. Applicants must have an bachelor's degree

76. Which is not part of job analysis?

    a. Selecting jobs to analyze

    b. Collecting data from incumbents

    c. Writing job descriptions

    d. Designing jobs

77. What is the main purpose of the Davis-Bacon Act of 1931?

    a. Requires federal contractors to implement affirmative action plans

    b. Prohibits discrimination on the basis of age over 50

    c. Requires certain federal contractors to pay a prevailing wage to employees

    d. Requires the payment of overtime to non-exempt employees

78. Which law protects employees covered by private pension programs?

    a. Employee Retirement Income Security Act

    b. Fair Credit Reporting Act

    c. Tax Reform Act of 1986

    d. Retirement Act

79. The National Labor Relations Act was enacted in:

    a. 1910

    b. 1935

    c. 1950

    d. 1999

80. An organization's mission statement includes:

    a. A statement of purpose

    b. The strategic plan

    c. The staffing model

    d. All of the above

81. Which union security clause requires workers to join a union?

    a. Closed shop

    b. Union shop

    c. Open shop

    d. Agency shop

82. How long does an employee have to file a complaint of discrimination with the EEOC?

    a. 30 days

    b. 90 days

    c. 180 days

    d. 365 days

83. According to the FLSA, which would be calculated toward overtime pay?

    a. A traffic jam causes the employee to get home an hour late

    b. The employee takes 3 days of paid vacation.

    c. The employee travels from home to a work site in response to an emergency

    d. The employee is on call but is able to conduct personal business

84. Which is not a requirement of the Americans with Disabilities Act (ADA)?

    a. Newly built public facilities must be accessible to people with disabilities

    b. Buildings financed with public funds must be accessible to people with disabilities

    c. Employers may ask applicants to disclose their disabilities to determine if an accommodation will need to be made

    d. Employers with more than 15 employees are required to provide reasonable accommodations to employees with disabilities

85. Which is <u>not</u> an important feature of new hire onboarding?

    a. Determining job satisfaction

    b. Training staff on company policies and procedures

    c. Providing a tour of the facilities

    d. Integrating new employees into the organizational culture

86. Which learning domains influence behavior?

    a. Skills

    b. Attitude

    c. Knowledge

    d. All of the above

87. What is a legal theory that makes employers liable for a harmful act if the employer knew about the employee's potential to cause harm?

    a. Reckless hiring

    b. Negligent hiring

    c. Liable hiring

    d. Risky hiring

88. What is the planned elimination of personnel to streamline operations?

    a. Acquisition

    b. Consolidation

    c. Termination

    d. Downsizing

89. **What occurs when a neutral employment policy has a disproportionately negative effect on minorities?**

    a. Adverse impact

    b. Disparate impact

    c. Discriminatory practice

    d. Personal bias

90. **An election has just been held in a bargaining unit. Of the employees who voted, 85% voted for the union. However, only 55% of those who voted are actually dues-paying members of the union. Which employees does the union represent?**

    a. Only the dues-paying members

    b. All who voted for the union

    c. All who voted for or against the union

    d. All employees in the bargaining unit

91. **Which law governs collective bargaining for federal employees?**

    a. National Labor Relations Act

    b. Wagner Act

    c. Civil Service Reform Act

    d. Taft-Hartley Act

92. **Americans working for an American company in Germany are referred to as:**

    a. Expatriates

    b. Host country nationals

    c. External immigrants

    d. Undocumented workers

93. Which are important activities in strategic planning?

    a. External scan

    b. Internal scan

    c. SWOT analysis

    d. All of the above

94. An interview process in which identical questions are asked of each candidate in the same order is called:

    a. Structured

    b. Unstructured

    c. EEO requirement

    d. Open ended

95. What type of compensation is an annual bonus?

    a. Time-based

    b. Direct

    c. Indirect

    d. Equitable

96. A progressive discipline is:

    a. A "zero tolerance" policy

    b. System of discrimination in disciplining employees

    c. A series of disciplinary actions that results in more severe punishment

    d. Required under the FLSA

97. According to Herzberg's theory, which of the following is a motivation factor?

    a. Personal growth

    b. Relationships with coworkers

    c. Job security

    d. Work environment

98. Which of the following are funding models of insurance?

    a. Self-funded

    b. Fully insured

    c. Both A and B

    d. None of the above

99. If an employee files a grievance, who typically handles it first?

    a. Supervisor

    b. President/CEO

    c. Arbitrator

    d. Union steward

100. What is <u>not</u> an example of a wellness program?

    a. Smoking cessation program

    b. Profit sharing

    c. Weight loss program

    d. Employee Assistance Program

101. Which restructuring practice broadens job scope by expanding the tasks it performs?

    a. Job rotation

    b. Job elimination

    c. Delegation

    d. Job enlargements

102. What is a payment given to employees who are laid off at no fault of their own?

    a. Life insurance

    b. Unemployment compensation

    c. Temporary pay

    d. Variable pay

103. What is an appropriate response by employers to sexual harassment complaints?

    a. Policy against sexual harassment

    b. Regular training of employees on sexual harassment

    c. Investigating complaints

    d. All of the above

104. Which law prohibits mandatory retirement based on an employee's age?

    a. Americans with Disabilities Act

    b. Genetic Information Nondiscrimination Act

    c. Age Discrimination in Employment Act

    d. Fair Labor Standards Act

105. A performance evaluation is also called:

a. Performance appraisal

b. Write-up

c. Progressive discipline

d. Informal feedback

106. Someone who is paid below the established pay range of a job is considered:

a. Green-circled

b. Red-circled

c. Purple-circled

d. Non-circled

107. Salary compression occurs when:

a. Employees are paid below the market rate

b. Employees in the same job receive the same salary

c. The starting salaries for new hires outpace year-to-year raises for existing staff

d. International workers earn less than others due to cost of living

108. The level of probability that an organization may be exposed to a hazard or loss:

a. Risk

b. Adverse impact

c. Vulnerability

d. Loss analysis

109. Which of the following is true under ADEA?

    a. A company may not set a retirement age

    b. A company may discontinue pension accruals for employees over age 62

    c. An employer may terminate an employee over 40 for poor performance

    d. It is against the law to require employees to be over 18

110. A company wants to understand the attitudes of employees in a short amount of time. Which method would be most appropriate?

    a. Observation

    b. In-person interview

    c. Questionnaire

    d. Hearsay

111. According to the ADA, a job description should list the essential functions of a job:

    a. In order of percentage of time spent on a task

    b. In order of importance

    c. In no order at all

    d. In alphabetical order

112. Which of the following laws protects people with physical or mental limitations from discrimination?

    a. FMLA

    b. ADA

    c. ADEA

    d. ERISA

113. What is a term used to describe when a qualified white male is denied an opportunity because preference is given to a member of a protected minority group?

    a. Reasonable accommodation

    b. Unfair employment practice

    c. Hostile work environment

    d. Reverse discrimination

114. Which of the following is considered indirect compensation?

    a. Use of a company cell phone

    b. Short-term disability insurance

    c. 401(k) matching contributions

    d. All of the above

115. *Quid pro quo* refers to:

    a. Sexual harassment

    b. Workplace accommodations

    c. Orientation

    d. Whistleblowing

116. A workweek in which a full week's work is completed in fewer days is called:

    a. Compressed workweek

    b. Telecommuting

    c. Job sharing

    d. Work-life balance

117. Which of the following is <u>not</u> an internal recruitment activity?

    a. Employee referrals

    b. Job posting on a website

    c. Job rotation

    d. Promoting from within

118. If your state minimum wage is higher than the federal minimum wage, how much are you required to pay employees at minimum?

    a. State minimum wage

    b. Federal minimum wage

    c. Average of state and federal minimum wages

    d. None of the above

119. Right-to-work laws allow states to:

    a. Ensure all citizens retain their job

    b. Require binding arbitration for disputes

    c. Require union membership at any company

    d. Prohibit compulsory union membership

120. Collective bargaining in which unions negotiate pay and working conditions similar to those that exist within the industry is referred to as:

    a. Multiple bargaining

    b. Parallel bargaining

    c. Coordinated bargaining

    d. Market bargaining

121. Which of the following decisions can be made on the basis of employee complaints?

    a. Employees can be reassigned to other departments.

    b. Managers can be fired.

    c. The company can identify areas where improvements may be needed

    d. Management can hire more staff.

122. Which is not a stage of the organizational life cycle?

    a. Birth

    b. Growth

    c. Maturity

    d. Death

123. The Occupational Safety and Health Act (OSHA) was enacted in:

    a. 1912

    b. 1960

    c. 1970

    d. 1986

124. An employee with HIV/AIDS who can perform essential functions of her job and is not a threat to the safety of other employees is protected by:

    a. EEOC

    b. FLSA

    c. ADA

    d. ADEA

125. An informal process of dispute resolution used by the EEOC is called:

    a. Employment at will

    b. Conciliation

    c. Mandated benefits

    d. Reconciliation

126. Which of the following information is typically not included in a job description?

    a. List of responsibilities

    b. FLSA status

    c. Required skills

    d. Company history

127. Which of the following does not usually affect recruitment planning?

    a. Government regulations

    b. Demographics of the workforce

    c. Available labor pool

    d. Location of the organization

128. A compensation philosophy that determines the value of the person's job in the organization and in the market is called:

    a. Market-based pay

    b. Pay for the person

    c. Pay for the job

    d. Equitable pay

129. Which agency oversees public sector labor relations?

a. National Labor Relations Board

b. Department of Labor

c. Federal Labor Relations Council

d. OFCCP

130. Which one is not a characteristic of an independent contractor?

a. They can work offsite

b. They have flexibility to set their own work schedules

c. They have an indefinite relationship with the employer

d. They must use their own work tools

131. Which is <u>not</u> a benefit of training?

a. Reduced profits

b. Reduction in errors

c. Reduction in turnover

d. Improved productivity

132. Which of the following best describes mentoring?

a. Providing feedback to a subordinate regarding his/her performance on the job

b. A professional relationship between two people that involves advice and support

c. Training a classroom of new hires on a product or service

d. Shadowing a person to learn his or her job

133. A manager only hires young women as waitresses. This is an example of:

    a. Disparate treatment

    b. Adverse impact

    c. Harassment

    d. Fair employment practice

134. How long do employers have to verify an employee's eligibility to work in the US?

    a. 1 day

    b. 3 days

    c. 7 days

    d. 14 days

135. What should be completed before writing a job description?

    a. Candidate interview

    b. Job analysis

    c. Downsizing

    d. Restructuring

136. A forced distribution method of rating employees does which of the following:

    a. Rates employees across a standard distribution

    b. Rank employees in order of productivity

    c. Distributes 360 surveys to the employee's peers

    d. Makes the employee rate him/herself

137. State "right to work" laws prohibit which of the following?

   a. Union shops

   b. Termination of employment

   c. Unfair labor practices

   d. Formation of unions

138. Succession planning is important because it:

   a. Ensures that key roles in the company will not be vacant

   b. Provides feedback for all employees

   c. Requires managers to go through training

   d. Controls the company's operating budget

139. With respect to nondiscrimination laws, which of the following is true?

   a. Federal laws trump state laws

   b. Employers must follow the law that provides the greatest employee protection

   c. State laws trump federal laws

   d. None of the above

140. Strategic planning is centered around the organization's:

   a. Staffing plan

   b. Mission statement

   c. Needs analysis

   d. Competitor data

141. Which of the following questions should an employer not ask its applicants?

    a. Are you able to perform the essential functions of the job with or without reasonable accommodation?

    b. Are you able to work on Sundays?

    c. Are you a US citizen?

    d. Are you over 18 years old?

142. Workers' Compensation is regulated by which body?

    a. State government

    b. Department of Labor

    c. OFCCP

    d. NLRB

143. The ADEA prohibits discrimination for which age groups?

    a. Over 18 years old

    b. Between 21 – 65 years old

    c. Between 40-65 years old

    d. Over 40 years old

144. Which of the following is examined during an environmental scan?

    a. Turnover rate

    b. Economic factors

    c. Employee complaints

    d. Organizational charts

145. Which of the following questions may an employer ask an applicant?

   a. Do you speak English fluently?

   b. What race are you?

   c. Are you married?

   d. Do you have a disability?

146. What did the McDonnell-Douglas Corp v. Green case establish?

   a. Adverse impact

   b. Unfair employment practices

   c. Disparate treatment

   d. Pregnancy nondiscrimination

147. Career planning focuses on the needs of whom?

   a. Employees

   b. Managers

   c. The organization

   d. The owners

148. Which concept recognizes that employee productivity is directly related to job satisfaction?

   a. HR management

   b. Strategic planning

   c. Human relations

   d. Performance management

149. **Which motivational theory states that people are motivated by rewards?**

    a. Equity theory

    b. Expectancy theory

    c. Alderfer's ERG theory

    d. Motivation-hygiene theory

150. **An audit of the services and costs billed by healthcare providers is called:**

    a. Claims analysis

    b. Utilization review

    c. Performance guarantee

    d. Pay for performance

Answer Key

1. C	31. A	61. A	91. C	121. C
2. A	32. A	62. C	92. A	122. D
3. D	33. B	63. D	93. D	123. C
4. C	34. B	64. B	94. A	124. C
5. A	35. D	65. B	95. B	125. B
6. C	36. A	66. D	96. C	126. D
7. B	37. B	67. B	97. A	127. B
8. A	38. C	68. A	98. C	128. C
9. C	39. C	69. C	99. A	129. C
10. D	40. A	70. A	100. B	130. C
11. A	41. C	71. B	101. D	131. A
12. C	42. B	72. C	102. B	132. B
13. D	43. D	73. D	103. D	133. A
14. C	44. B	74. D	104. C	134. B
15. B	45. A	75. B	105. A	135. B
16. D	46. B	76. D	106. A	136. B
17. C	47. D	77. C	107. C	137. A
18. B	48. A	78. A	108. A	138. A
19. B	49. A	79. B	109. C	139. B
20. C	50. D	80. A	110. C	140. B
21. B	51. C	81. B	111. B	141. C
22. B	52. D	82. C	112. B	142. A
23. A	53. B	83. C	113. D	143. D
24. A	54. C	84. C	114. D	144. B
25. D	55. C	85. A	115. A	145. A
26. C	56. C	86. D	116. A	146. C
27. A	57. A	87. B	117. B	147. A
28. C	58. A	88. D	118. A	148. C
29. A	59. C	89. A	119. D	149. B
30. C	60. D	90. D	120. B	150. B

Table of References

"About the Law." *United States Department of Health and Human Services*. Web. 21 Mar. 2014.
    <http://www.hhs.gov/healthcare/rights/>.

"All About Strategic Planning." *Free Management Library*. Web. 15 Feb. 2014.
    <http://managementhelp.org/strategicplanning/index.htm#anchor1234>.

"Basic Overview of Organizational Life Cycles." *Basic Overview of Organizational Life Cycles*.
    Web. 7 Mar. 2014. <http://managementhelp.org/organizations/life-cycles.htm>.

"Careers in Human Resource Management." *Society for Human Resource Management*. Web. 1
    Mar. 2014.
    <http://www.shrm.org/Communities/StudentPrograms/Pages/careersinHRM.aspx>.

"Centralized Vs. Decentralized Organizational Structure." *Small Business*. Web. 7 Mar. 2014.
    <http://smallbusiness.chron.com/centralized-vs-decentralized-organizational-
    structure-2785.html>.

"Choose Your Business Structure | SBA.gov." *Choose Your Business Structure | SBA.gov*. Web.
    22 Feb. 2014. <http://www.sba.gov/category/navigation-structure/starting-managing-
    business/starting-business/choose-your-business-stru>.

"Core Leadership Theories." *Leadership Skills From MindTools.com*. Web. 8 Mar. 2014.
    <http://www.mindtools.com/pages/article/leadership-theories.htm>.

"Division of labor." *Wikipedia*. Wikimedia Foundation, n.d. Web. 17 Mar. 2014.
    <http://en.wikipedia.org/wiki/Division_of_labour>.

"Employee handbook." *Wikipedia*. Wikimedia Foundation, n.d. Web. 2 Mar. 2014.
    <http://en.wikipedia.org/wiki/Employee_handbook>.

"French and Raven's Forms of Power." *ChangingMinds.org*. Web. 19 Feb. 2014.
    <http://changingminds.org/explanations/power/french_and_raven.htm>.

"Going Global: Managing the Challenges of Global Compensation." *Talent Management*. Web.
    18 Mar. 2014.
    <http://talentmgt.com/articles/view/going_global_managing_the_challenges_of_globa
    l_compensation>.

"Handling Complaints and Grievances." *Edward Lowe Foundation*. Web. 19 Feb. 2014.
    <http://edwardlowe.org/digital-library/handling-complaints-and-grievances/>.

"Health Insurance Portability and Accountability Act." *Wikipedia*. Wikimedia Foundation, n.d.
    Web. 18 Feb. 2014.
    <http://en.wikipedia.org/wiki/Health_Insurance_Portability_and_Accountability_Act>.

"Henry Mintzberg." *ProvenModels*. Web. 7 Mar. 2014. <http://www.provenmodels.com/17/six-coordination-mechanisms/henry-mintzberg>.

"Hiring." *U.S. Department of Labor*. Web. 11 Mar. 2014. <http://www.dol.gov/dol/topic/hiring/affirmativeact.htm>.

"HR in Mergers and Acquisitions." *OrgChart.net*. Web. 22 Mar. 2014. <http://www.orgchart.net/wiki/HR_in_Mergers_and_Acquisitions>.

"Human Capital Management Reference Materials." *U.S. Office of Personnel Management*. Web. 18 Feb. 2014. <http://www.opm.gov/policy-data-oversight/human-capital-management/reference-materials/strategic-alignment/>.

"Human Resources Certification Institute." *HRCI.org*. Web. 22 Feb. 2014. <http://www.hrci.org/>.

"Kurt Lewin Biography (1890-1947)." *About.com Psychology*. Web. 11 Mar. 2014. <http://psychology.about.com/od/profilesofmajorthinkers/p/bio_lewin.htm>.

"Laws Enforced by EEOC." *EEOC*. Web. 11 Mar. 2014. <http://www.eeoc.gov/laws/statutes/>.

"Learning Styles." *Baltimore County Public Schools*. Web. 1 Apr. 2014. <http://www.bcps.org/offices/lis/models/tips/styles.html>.

"Lewin's Leadership Styles." *About.com Psychology*. Web. 7 Mar. 2014. <http://psychology.about.com/od/leadership/a/leadstyles.htm>.

"Maslow's hierarchy of needs." *Wikipedia*. Wikimedia Foundation, n.d. Web. 7 Mar. 2014. <http://en.wikipedia.org/wiki/Maslow's_hierarchy_of_needs>.

"Mental Health Parity." *US Department of Labor*. Web. 19 Feb. 2014. <http://www.dol.gov/ebsa/mentalhealthparity/>.

"Methods of Training Employees." *Employee Training HQ*. Web. 19 Feb. 2014. <http://employeetraininghq.com/methods-of-training-employees/>.

"National Whistleblowers Center." *National Whistleblowers Center*. Web. 7 Apr. 2014. <http://www.whistleblowers.org/index.php?option=com_content&task=view&id=27>.

"Organizational Architecture." *Wikipedia*. Wikimedia Foundation, n.d. Web. 1 Mar. 2014. <http://en.wikipedia.org/wiki/Organizational_architecture#Design>.

"Organizational Life Cycle." *Inc.com*. Web. 2 Mar. 2014. <http://www.inc.com/encyclopedia/organizational-life-cycle.html>.

"Organizational structure." *Wikipedia*. Wikimedia Foundation, n.d. Web. 6 Mar. 2014. <http://en.wikipedia.org/wiki/Organizational_structure>.

"Organizing Human Resource Issues for Business Continuity." *Disaster Recovery Journal*. Web. 1 Mar. 2014. <http://www.drj.com/drworld/content/w3_021.htm>.

"Pay Structures." *Salary.com*. Web. 19 Feb. 2014. <http://www.salary.com/pay-structures/>.

"Reforming Corporate America." *Pepperdine University*. Web. 28 Feb. 2014. <http://gbr.pepperdine.edu/2010/08/reforming-corporate-america/>.

"Reorganization." *OrgChart.net*. Web. 7 Mar. 2014. <http://www.orgchart.net/wiki/Reorganization>.

"Required Employee Benefits | SBA.gov." *Small Business Association*. Web. 27 Feb. 2014. <http://www.sba.gov/content/required-employee-benefits>.

"Sarbanes Oxley Act." *Wikipedia*. Wikimedia Foundation, n.d. Web. 7 Mar. 2014. <http://en.wikipedia.org/wiki/Sarbanes_Oxley_Act>.

"Six Main Functions of a Human Resource Department." *Small Business*. Web. 7 Mar. 2014. <http://smallbusiness.chron.com/six-main-functions-human-resource-department-60693.html>.

"Span of Control: What factors should determine how many direct reports a manager has." *Society for Human Resource Management*. Web. 18 Mar. 2014. <http://www.shrm.org/TemplatesTools/hrqa/Pages/Whatfactorsshoulddeterminehowmanydirectreportsamanagerhas.aspx>.

"Speak Easy: The Importance of Ongoing Employee Communications." *Go2HR.ca*. Web. 18 Mar. 2014. <https://www.go2hr.ca/articles/speak-easy-importance-ongoing-employee-communications>.

"Succession Planning." *Office of Personnel Management*. Web. 18 Mar. 2014. <https://www.opm.gov/policy-data-oversight/human-capital-management/reference-materials/leadership-knowledge-management/successionplanning.pdf>.

"The Age Discrimination in Employment Act of 1967." *EEOC*. Web. 6 Mar. 2014. <http://www.eeoc.gov/laws/statutes/adea.cfm>.

"The Equal Pay Act of 1963." *EEOC*. Web. 5 Mar. 2014. <http://www.eeoc.gov/laws/statutes/epa.cfm>.

"The Pregnancy Discrimination Act of 1978." *EEOC*. Web. 6 Mar. 2014. <http://www.eeoc.gov/laws/statutes/pregnancy.cfm>.

"The Role of Human Resources in Mergers & Acquisitions." *Small Business*. Web. 4 Mar. 2014. <http://smallbusiness.chron.com/role-human-resources-mergers-acquisitions-23589.html>.

"Title VII of the Civil Rights Act of 1964." *EEOC*. Web. 6 Mar. 2014.
    <http://www.eeoc.gov/laws/statutes/titlevii.cfm>.

"Titles I and V of the Americans with Disabilities Act of 1990 (ADA)." *EEOC*. Web. 7 Mar. 2014.
    <http://www.eeoc.gov/laws/statutes/ada.cfm>.

"Types of Discipline Used in the Workplace." *Everyday Life*. Web. 21 Mar. 2014.
    <http://everydaylife.globalpost.com/types-discipline-used-workplace-2647.html>.

"U.S. Bureau of Labor Statistics." *U.S. Bureau of Labor Statistics*. U.S. Bureau of Labor Statistics,
    n.d. Web. 6 Apr. 2014. <http://www.bls.gov/>.

"U.S. Bureau of Labor Statistics." *U.S. Bureau of Labor Statistics*. U.S. Bureau of Labor Statistics,
    n.d. Web. 6 Mar. 2014. <http://www.bls.gov/>.

"What are Employee Privacy Rights?" *Small Business*. Web. 7 Feb. 2014.
    <http://smallbusiness.chron.com/employee-privacy-rights-1239.html>.

"What Are the Functions of Payroll vs. Human Resource?" *Business & Entrepreneurship*. Web.
    18 Mar. 2014. <http://yourbusiness.azcentral.com/functions-payroll-vs-human-
    resource-7956.html>.

"What is Total Rewards?" *WorldAtWork*. Web. 1 Mar. 2014.
    <https://www.worldatwork.org/aboutus/html/aboutus-whatis.jsp>.

"What Is Transformational Leadership?" *About.com Psychology*. Web. 27 Feb. 2014.
    <http://psychology.about.com/od/leadership/a/transformational.htm>.

"Workforce Planning." *OrgChart.net*. Web. 19 Feb. 2014.
    <http://www.orgchart.net/wiki/Workforce_Planning>.

CPSIA information can be obtained at www.ICGtesting.com
Printed in the USA
BVOW09s0153010915

415147BV00005B/87/P